NOTES
ON
PUSHTU GRAMMAR

NOTES
ON
PUSHTU GRAMMAR

A. D. COX

TOGETHER WITH AN
APPENDIX
CONTAINING ALL THE RECENT "SENTENCES"
AND "PASSAGES FOR TRANSLATION"

GYAN

Published by

Gyan Publishing House
5, Ansari Road
Daryaganj, New Delhi-110002
Phone: 011-47034999, 9811692060
E-mail: books@gyanbooks.com

Distribution Network
gyanbooks.com
India, USA, Canada, UK, Australia, France

ISBN : 978-81-212-4481-7 (PB)
First Published, London, 1911

2nd Impression 2020

Printed at: Gyan Press, Delhi.

Notes on Pushtu Grammar
Author: A. D. Cox

NOTES
ON
PUSHTU GRAMMAR

BY

MAJOR A. D. COX
69TH PUNJABIS

TOGETHER WITH AN

APPENDIX

CONTAINING ALL THE RECENT "SENTENCES" AND "PASSAGES FOR TRANSLATION" SET BY THE PESHAWAR BOARD OF EXAMINERS.

LONDON
CROSBY LOCKWOOD & SON
7, STATIONERS' HALL COURT, LUDGATE HILL

1911

PREFACE.

THE accompanying book does not profess to be an exhaustive treatise on Pushtu Grammar. It is rather the result of a collection of notes made while reading with Mr. Mian Sami ud-Din, Barrister-at-law (Middle Temple), and Munshi Ajab Khan.

It is published in the hope that various difficulties which present themselves to beginners may be explained—difficulties which either have not been explained in any hitherto published Grammar (as far as the Author knows), or which, having been made clear in Major Bellew's Grammar, are still a stumbling-block to students, as that book has been for many years out of print and unobtainable.

The chief objects aimed at in the present work have been—

(1) to simplify the Declension of Nouns;

(2) to give a list of Adjectives which form their Feminine Singular and Masculine Plural in ways which would involve complicated rules being invented to account for them, only to lead to lists of exceptions; and

(3) to show diagrammatically how the Conjugation of Pushtu Verbs can be reduced to a system.

As this last object is the chief feature of and apology for publishing these Notes, an explanation of the same must be offered.

The Verb in its simple form, i.e. the Infinitive, is regarded as the founder of a family, having a number of sons (Columns 1, 2, 3, 4, and sometimes 5; see Table C and pages 40 to 63); the sons in their turn having descendants of their own, the eldest son (Column 1) having descendants by two wives (Columns 1 and 1A). The Diagram, Table C, is therefore drawn out after the manner of a genealogical tree.

The commonest Verbs in the language are the most irregular, and they have been conjugated out in full; yet, in spite of their irregularities, it will be seen that they too conform in a marked degree to the scheme.

Many Verbs have one or more irregular tenses. Lists of such Verbs, showing their irregularities, have been given. When these have been learnt, all the Verbs can be conjugated out according to rule by merely placing the irregular tense in its proper place on the diagram: we shall then find that all tenses subsequently derived from these irregular tenses are themselves perfectly regularly formed.

It may be objected that by this scheme moods have been hopelessly mixed up. This is so, and no attempt is made to disguise the fact.

The Author's best thanks are due to his friend Mr. Mian Sami ud-Din, who has never grudged giving much of his valuable time in helping and advising while the Notes were in an embryonic form; as well as to his well-known brother, Munshi Abd ul-Razack, for suggestions and help. Nor can anyone who attempts to write anything on Pushtu Grammar fail to acknowledge his indebtedness to Bellew's standard work.

The Author is only too well aware of many shortcomings in this work, and would welcome any suggestions for correcting or making it more useful should circumstances show that a second edition would be welcome.

A. D. COX,
69th Punjabis.
(Attached 21st Punjabis.)

BANNU,
July, 1911.

TABLE OF CONTENTS.

	PAGES
INTRODUCTION	
The Alphabet	1–4
Parts of Speech	4

	PARA.
CHAPTER I.	
Nouns	1–16
Verbal Nouns	17, 70
Pronouns	18–33
Adjectives	34–41
„ Comparison of	42–44
Abstract Nouns	46
Numerals	47–59
CHAPTER II.	
Verbs	60–119
„ Derivative or Compound	62–68
Moods	69–78
Tenses, Formation of	79, 80
Irregular Verbs	84, 86, 90–108
Original Infinitives	84, 87
Defective Auxiliary Verb "To Be"	89
Construction of Sentence containing Past Tense of Transitive Verb	110–117
On the use of شته and دي	120
On the difference between دي and وِي	121
Prohibition and Negation	122–125
Continued Action	126
On the use of Past Tense in a Narrative	127
Two verbs joined by "and"	128
Oratio Obliqua and Oratio Recta	129
On the use of تلل and راتلل	130
"Possession," how expressed	131

CHAPTER III.

	PARA.
Adverbs	132–139
„ of Time	132
„ of Place	133
„ of Manner	134
„ of Degree	135
„ of Cause	136
„ of Order	137
„ of Affirmation	138
„ of Negation	139
Conjunctions	140
Prepositions	141, 142
Interjections	143
Calendar	144–153
Greetings	154–156

INDEX.

PARAS.

"About," with a number 52
Abstract Nouns 46
Active Agent 5 (6), 80
Adjectives 34–41
,, comparison of 42–44
,, declension of 36–39
,, formation of Feminine. .36–39
,, indeclinable, خپل . . 28
,, irregular feminines of . 37, 39
,, Pronominal 33
,, qualifying two or more nouns 35
,, Verbal 45
Adverbs. 132–139
,, of Affirmation 138
,, Cause 136
,, Degree 135
,, Manner 134
,, Negation 139
,, Order 137
,, Place 133
,, Time 132
Agent to be expressed in sentence containing Past tense of Transitive Verb 115
Alphabet, Letters of Pushtu . pages 1–4
Arabic forms of letters. . . . pages 1–4
Article, Definite and Indefinite .page 4
Auxiliary Verb (Defective) To Be . 89
,, ,, (Irregular) To Become 90
,, ,, ,, To Make . 91

PARAS.

Calendar 144–153
Cases of Nouns 1, 9, 10, 11, 14
,, formations of. 15
Causal Verbs 88
Comparison of Adjectives 42–44
Conditional Mood 74
,, Pluperfect 75
,, Sentences 75, 76
Continued action, how expressed . . 126
Conjunctions 140
Correlative Pronouns 31

Date 152, 153
Day, difference between Christian and Mohammedan 151
Day and Night, subdivisions of . 148–150
Demonstrative Pronouns 26
Difference between Male and Female, how shown . 5
,, ,, دي and وي. . . 121
Diminutives 16
Distribution, how expressed . . . 53

Feminines of Adjectives, how formed .36–39
Feminine Nouns, classes of . . . 10
,, ,, how declined . . 10
,, ,, how formed . . . 5
,, irregular, of Nouns . . . 6
Fractions 47

PARAS.

Genders of Nouns, how determined . 2, 3
,, ,, general rule for . 3
,, ,, difference in Singular and Plural . 7
,, ,, difference in, how shown . . . 3, 5
Genitive Case; long and short forms, difference between 23
Gerund 80
Greetings 154–156

Imperative Mood 72
Indeclinable Adjective, خيل 28
Indefinite Pronouns 32
Indicative Mood 71, 80
Infinitive Mood 70, 80
,, ,, used as Noun . . 70
Inflected cases of Nouns 1
,, ,, Personal Pronouns 20, 22
Interjections 143
Interrogative Pronouns 30

Masculine Nouns, classes of . . . 11
,, ,, how declined . . 11
Months of Hindu year 145
,, Mohammedan year . . . 144
Moods 69–78
Multiplication, how expressed . . 54
Multitude, ,, ,, . . 55

Narrative, Past tense in . . . 127
Negation and Prohibition . . . 122–125
Nouns, Abstract 46

PARAS.

Nouns, cases of 1, 14, 15
,, gender of 2–4
,, having same form in Nom. Singular and Nom. Plural . . 13
,, numbers of, Formation of Plural 8
,, expressing Rank or Dignity regarded as adjectives when used with Verbs 67
,, Singular in form but requiring Plural Verb (Remarks Column) 10
,, Verbal 70
Numerals 47–59
,, Declension of Cardinal Numbers . . . 51
,, ,, ,, Ordinal .. 58, 59
,, Feminine of Cardinal .. 51
,, ,, ,, Ordinal .. 57
,, Formation of Ordinal ,, 57

Object of Transitive Verb must be expressed 118
Obsolete letter . . . . . . page 3
Optative Mood 123
Oratio Obliqua and Oratio Recta . . 129
Ordinal Numbers, Declension of . .58, 59
,, ,, Feminine of . . 57
,, ,, Formation of . . 57
Original Infinitives 60, 84, 87

Parts of Speech . . . . . . page 4
Passive Voice, how formed . . . 62
,, ,, use of 61
Past Participle 80

PARAS.

Past tense of Transitive Verb, Construction of sentence containing . . . 110–117
,, in Narrative 127
Personal Pronouns 19–25
Plurals, formations of; Adjectives. . 36–39
,, ,, Nouns . 8, 10–13
,, ,, Numerals . 58
,, ,, Pronouns. 19, 20
,, irregular 12
Possession, how expressed 131
Possessive Pronouns 23, 28
Potential Mood 78, 80
Prepositions. 141, 142
Prohibition and Negation . . . 122–125
Pronouns, Correlative 31
,, Demonstrative 26
,, Indefinite 32
,, Interrogative . . . 30
,, Personal 19–25
,, ,, declension of . . 20
,, ,, prefixed to Verbs 24 (2)
,, ,, various forms oblique cases take 24
,, Possessive 28
,, ,, position of . . 23
,, Reflexive 29
,, Relative 27
Pronominal Adjectives 33

Reflexive Pronouns 29
Relative Pronouns 27

Seasons 146
Speech, Parts of . . . . . page 4

PARAS.

Subjunctive Mood 73, 80
Suffixes distinguishing the various Persons in Verbs 81

Tenses, formation of 79, 80

Universality, how expressed . . . 56
Use of شته and دي 120
Use of تلل and راتلل 130

Verbal Adjectives 45
,, Nouns 70
Verbs 60–119
,, Causal 88
,, Defective Auxiliary, To Be . 89
,, Derivative (or Compound) . . 62–68
,, ,, how formed . . 62
,, endings of 60
,, ending in يدل 83, 84
,, ,, تل 85, 86
,, having peculiar construction in Past tenses 119
,, Irregular Auxiliary, To Become, كيدل . . 90
,, ,, ,, To Do, or Make, كول 91
,, Irregular, Lists of . 84, 86, 107, 108
,, ,, To Go, تلل . . . 92
,, ,, To Come, راتلل . . 93
,, joined by "and" . . . 128
,, Passive, how formed . . 62
,, ,, when used 62
,, روانيدل example of Compound Verb (كيدل with Adjective) 94

PARAS.

Verbs, روانول example of Compound Verb (کول with Adjective) . 95
„ گرزيدل (intransitive) . . . 96
„ لويدل „ . . . 97
„ استول (transitive) 98
„ بيول or بوتلل (defective transitive) 99
„ وړل „ „ 100
„ راوړل 101
„ نيول (transitive) 102
„ کېښودل „ 103
Verbs, ويستل (transitive) . . . 104
„ راخکل „ 105
„ ويل „ 106
„ which do not prefix و in any tense . . . . Note (4) 80

Week, Days of 147
"What"—referring to date . . . 153
Written character ٓ . . . . . page 4

ERRATA.

Page 38, paragraph 87, lines 9 and 10, *for* to travel backwards and forwards *read:* (1) to drive pack animals; (2) to drive a carriage; (3) to use weapons.

Page 40, column 1A, line 7, *add* 89.

Page 67, paragraph 112, line 1, *for* 111 *read* 110.

NOTES ON PUSHTU GRAMMAR.

INTRODUCTION.

THE PUSHTU ALPHABET.

FORM.	NAME.	POWER.	EXAMPLES OF FORM.		
			Initial.	Medial.	Final.
ا	Ālif	a, long.	اصل	کار	تا
ب	Bé	b.	بل	سبق	قریب
پ	Pé	p.	پاک	سپيَ	اسپ
ت	Té	t, soft, dental, as in *the*.	ترل	دلته	ناست
ټ	Té	t, hard, as in *tea*.	ټيټ	پټيَ	کټ
ث	Sé	s, soft.	ثبوت	اکثر	بحث
ښ	Sé	s, as in *so* (frequently called "the Pushtu s").	ښوک	ښښول	هيښ
ږ	Zé	z ("the Pushtu z")	ږاي	نږه	وريږ
ج	Jim	j, as in *joy*.	جنيَ	بجذ	پنج
چ	Ché	ch, as in *church*.	چه	چيچل	کچ
ح	Hé	h aspirate, strongly marked.	حد	محتاج	تشريح
خ	Khé	kh, like *ch* in the word *loch*.	خير	تخم	يخ
د	Dāl	d.	دنگر	بيدار	حد
ډ	Dhāl	d, hard.	ډير	هډو	گډ
ذ	Zāl	z, as in *zeal*.	ذهن	عذر	کاغذ
ر	Ré	r, as in *run*.	رنځ	کړل	تير

THE PUSHTU ALPHABET (*continued*).

FORM.	NAME.	POWER.	EXAMPLES OF FORM.		
			Initial.	Medial.	Final.
ړ	Rré	rr, hard.	ړچيدل	رغړم	کړ
ز	Zé	z.	زنه	مزري	کوز
ژ	Jé	j, as in French *je*.	ژمې	خيژم	مونژ
ږ	Gé	g, as in *gay*.	ږيره	کږه	شپږ
س	Sin	s.	سُم	پسته	کس
ش	Shin	sh, as in *she*.	شل	پيشو	ويش
ښ	Khin	kh, hard, or sh, soft.	ښهر	آزميښت	کښ
ص	Swād	s, soft.	صاف	حصه	قميص
ض	Zwād	z.	ضرور	مضبوط	عرض
ط	Toë	t.	طرف	خطا	مضبوط
ظ	Zoë	z.	ظلم	حفاظت	حافظ
ع	'Ain	a, broad.	عجيب	طبيعت	طمع
غ	Ghain	gh, guttural.	غله	پيغله	بالغ
ف	Fé	f.	فساد	تفصيل	انصاف
ق	Qāf	qh.	قبول	رقعه	لايق
ک	Kāf	k.	کول	ليکل	شک
ګ	Gāf	g, as in *go*.	ګډوډ	تګي	تګ
ل	Lām	l.	لرې	ملا	کال
م	Mim	m.	منل	تمام	ځم
ن	Nūn	n.	نور	غني	شان
و	Wāo	o, ow, u, or w, according to the vowel-points.	ونه	نوک	خو
ه	Hé	h.	هلک	بهر	تره
ي	Yé	e, i, or y, according to the vowel-points.	يخ	نيم	سړی

The Pushtu alphabet contains 39 letters, of which 7 are purely Pushtu, viz.:—
ټ ځ څ ډ ړ ږ and ښ.

ټ ډ ړ correspond exactly to the Urdu letters ٹ ڈ and ڑ respectively.

څ has the same power as س.

ځ has the same power as ز.

ږ is pronounced as گ (*g*) by the Usafzais and certain other Pathans forming a numerical minority in the total of Pushtu speaking clans. All other Pathan clans pronounce this letter as if it were the equivalent of ژ (*j*).

Those Pathans who give ږ the same value as گ (*g*) pronounce ښ as if it were خ (*kh*), while all others give it the same power as ش (*sh*).

It is for this reason that the word "*Pushtu*" is frequently written "*Pukhtu.*"

ښ often immediately follows or precedes ک. In the former case it is silent; in the latter the two letters are sounded separately.

ڼ is an obsolete letter having the power *nr*. It is now written نړ.

The pronunciation of these two letters in combination is not easy to acquire, and must be learnt from a Pathan. The ړ is clipped and swallowed almost as soon as one begins to pronounce it.

ه is sometimes "perceptible" (hé zāhir) and sometimes "imperceptible" (hé khāfi). In the latter case, when at the end of a word, it is often dropped, and its place taken by the short vowel *zăwăr* (◌َ) written over the last letter of the word.

ي The power of this letter varies according to the vowel-points which accompany it.

Written thus :—يٖ its power is as in the French é.

ِي " " " " " i in *oui.*

ې " " is nearly equal to يٖ, but not quite so marked.

ئ " " is like y in *cry*.

Only when written as a final letter are the vowel-points given.

When ي is an initial letter its power is *y*.

When it is a medial letter its power varies, being sometimes é and sometimes i. There is nothing to guide one as to the correct pronunciation except knowledge of the language.

The three vowel-points known in Urdu as Zăbăr (ـَ), Zér (ـِ) and Pésh (ـُ) are called in Pushtu "*Zăwăr*," "*Zér*" and "*Pékh*" respectively.

"*Shad*" (شد)—the equivalent of the Urdu "*Tashdid*"—is used only in Arabic quotations. It never appears in a purely Pushtu word. When it is necessary to double a consonant in a Pushtu word, a dash like a *zăwăr* is made over the letter ; e.g. پـوَر.

Hamza (ء) placed above the second of two contiguous vowels indicates that the vowels are to be pronounced separately.

In writing Pushtu no "*Shikasta*" or broken hand should be used. The written and printed characters are therefore exactly alike.

The Arabic form لا (for لا) is frequent and correct.

The Arabic form of ر (ر) is also not uncommon.

Pushtu having comparatively recently been reduced to writing, one frequently meets the same word differently spelt; this is not to be wondered at, considering the number of letters in the alphabet which have the same, or almost the same, value.

PARTS OF SPEECH.

According to Persian and Arabic grammarians there are three parts of speech, viz., the Noun, the Verb, and the Particle. Pushtu follows the same rule.

The Noun comprises what in English would be called :—

Nouns (or Substantives).	Adjectives.
Verbal Nouns.	Abstract Nouns.
Pronouns.	Numerals.

The Verb as in English.

The Particle includes :—

Adverbs.	Prepositions.
Conjunctions.	Interjections.

There is no Definite or Indefinite Article in Pushtu corresponding to "*the*" and "*a*" or "*an*" of English. The Article is understood in the Noun.

If a Definite Article is required to differentiate a Noun, the Demonstrative Pronouns دغه, دا or هغه (para. 26) must be used.

If an Indefinite Article is required, then the Numeral يو (Mas.) or يوه (Fem.) is employed.

CHAPTER I.

NOUNS.

1. In Pushtu, Nouns have two Genders (Mas. and Fem.), two Numbers (Sing. and Plural), and eight Cases, viz. :—

Nominative.
Accusative.
Vocative.
Genitive.
Dative.
Ablative.
Locative.
Instrumental.

(Vocative. to Instrumental.) } "Inflected cases."

GENDER.

2. The Gender of Nouns is determined by :—

1. Their meaning, or
2. The termination of the Nominative Singular.

Thus :— ماما uncle (mother's brother).
تره (*thrā̆*) uncle (father's brother).
غازي fanatic.
مرئ (*marai-é*) slave.
ميلو bear.
ترور (*thrōr*) aunt.
غوايه bullock.

} sufficiently denote their genders by their meanings, so that the termination of the Nom. Sing. is immaterial.

3. As a *General Rule*, Nouns ending in ا, و, ه, ي or ئ are Feminine, and all others are Masculine.

4. Certain Nouns appear to be exceptions to this rule, because they are Feminine although ending in consonants. As a matter of fact they are not exceptions; the final ة has been generally dropped, though in many villages the words still retain their correct form. A few such words are:—

پلټن	a regiment, which correctly speaking should be				پلټنه
څرمن	a skin,	,,	,,	,,	څرمنه
لار	a road,	,,	,,	,,	لاره
مياشت	a month,	,,	,,	,,	مياشته
ورځ	a day,	,,	,,	,,	ورځه

They are therefore Feminine according to rule.

5. The difference between Male and Female may be shown in various ways.

(1.) By separate words.

پلار father.	مور mother.
ورور (*rōr*) brother.	خور sister.
ځوئ son.	لور daughter.
آس horse.	اسپه mare.

(2.) By the addition of the word نر (male) or ښځه (female) to words which are usually of common gender.

نر کارغه a crow (cock).	ښځه کارغه a crow (hen).

(3.) By adding ة to the Masculine.

ماشوم a male child.	ماشومه a female child.
غل a thief.	غله a female thief.
اوښ a camel.	اوښه a female camel.

(4.) Nouns which have a long vowel in the last syllable drop it before following the preceding rule.

پښتون a Pathan man.	پښتنه a Pathan woman.
چنغول a betrothed man.	چنغله an affianced woman.

(5.) Nouns which end in ې change it to ۍ.

سپې a dog.	سپۍ a bitch.

(6.) The Active Agent (see Table C, p. 34) changes ې into ي.

راتلونكې he who comes.	راتلونكي she who comes.

The difference in pronunciation is scarcely perceptible.

(7.) Masculine nouns ending in ي change this letter into ڼړه.

دوبي a washerman. — دوبڼړه a washerwoman.

موچي a shoemaker. — موچڼړه a shoemaker's wife.

Although the above is quite correct grammatically, yet in the use of the Feminine form there lurks an implied insult. دَ دوبي ښځه or دَ موچي ښځه can be used without offence.

6. The following Nouns have *Irregular Feminines*:—

آس a horse. — اسپه a mare.

پيسه a goat. — بيزه a "nanny" goat.

غوبه a cowherd. — غوبنه a cowherd's wife.

ميلو a bear. — ميلوګي a she-bear.

7. The following Nouns are Masculine in the Singular, and Feminine in the Plural:—

اشر[1] a Helping Party.[2] — اشري

تبر a family. — تبري

ډز a shot fired, or report of rifle. — ډزي

کمر a cliff. — کمري

کندر a hole dug by thieves to enter a house. — کندري

لښکر an army. — لښکري

The above plurals are irregularly formed.

NUMBER.

8. The formation of the Plural of Nouns will be most easily understood by reference to Columns 3 and 5 of the two following Tables (A and B).

It will be convenient to take the Feminine Nouns first, and the Masculine Nouns afterwards.

9. From Column 6 of the two Tables it will be noticed that final و is the distinguishing feature of the inflected cases Plural of ALL Nouns.

---

[1] اشر has also a regularly-formed plural اشرونه, which is Masculine.

[2] A "Helping Party" is a party of men called in to help in cutting crops, building a house, etc. The men receive no pay, but are given special food.

10. TABLE A. FEMININE NOUNS.

1	2	3	4	5	6	7
CLASS.	NOM. SING. ENDING IN:	EXAMPLE.	INFLECTED CASES SINGULAR.	NOM. PLURAL.	INFLECTED CASES PLURAL.	REMARKS.
I.	ا	بلا *a calamity.*	Remain unaltered.	Same as Nom. Sing.	Add و to Nom. Plur.: پہ بلاو کښِں *in calamities.*	The important exceptions to Class III. are the following Masculine Nouns:—
II.	و	پيشو *a cat.*	Remain unaltered.	Add گاني to Nom. Sing.: پيشوگاني *cats.*	Final ي of Nom. Plural becomes و: پيشوگانو ته *to cats.*	(Nom. Plural. / Inflected Cases Plural.) واده a marriage وادونه وادونو مارغه a bird مرغان مرغانو
III.	ﻫ	رساله *a cavalry regiment.*	Final ﻫ becomes ي: له رسالي نه *from the regiment.*	Final ﻫ of Nom. Sing. becomes ي: رسالي *cavalry regiments.*	Final ي of Nom. Plural becomes و: دَ رسالو *of the regiments.*	The following Nouns, though Singular in form, require a Plural Verb, and are inflected as Plural Nouns only:—
IV.	ي	نيکي *goodness.*	Final ي becomes ئي: دَ نيکئي *of goodness.*	Same as Nom. Sing.	Final ي becomes و.	اوبه water. مازغه brain.
V.	ئي	څپلئي *a sandal.*	Remain unaltered.	Same as Nom. Sing.	Final ئي becomes و: څپلو سره *with sandals.*	ساره cold. ماسته curds. شوده milk. وابنه grass. ريښم silk. ويښته hair.
VI.	a Consonant.	لار *a road.*	Add short vowel zér (ـِ): دَ لارِ *of the road.*	Same as Inflected Cases Singular.	Add و to Nom. Sing.: پہ لارو کښِں *in the roads.*	غارمه heat.

11. TABLE B. MASCULINE NOUNS.

1	2	3	4	5	6	7
Class.	Nom. Sing. ending in:	Example.	Inflected Cases Singular.	Nom. Plural.	Inflected Cases Plural.	Remarks.
I.	ي	سړي *a man.*	ي becomes ي: له سړي نه *from a man.*	Same as Inflected Cases Singular.	Final ي becomes و: دَ سړو *of men.*	مريځ, a slave, has Inflected Cases Plural مريو, which is really a contracted form of مريونو, from Nom. Plural مريونه.
II.	a Consonant, and denoting an Animate object.	مار *a snake.*	Remain unaltered.	Add ان to Nom. Sing.[1]: ماران *snakes.*	Add و to Nom. Plural: دَ مارانو *of snakes.*	مُلا, a priest, has two forms of Plural:
III.	a Consonant, and denoting an Inanimate object.	کور *a house.*	Remain unaltered.	Add ونه to Nom. Sing.[1]: کورونه *houses.*	Final ه of Nom. Plural becomes و: دَ کورونو *of houses.*	Nominative: مُلايان and مُلين; Inflected Cases: مُلايانو, مُلينو
IV.	a Consonant, and representing a Sound.	کرپ *a crack.*	Remain unaltered.	Add هار to Nom. Sing.: کرپهار *cracks.*	Add و to Nom. Plural: په کرپهارو کښې *in cracks.*	

[1] These are not very satisfactory rules, for many Nouns which, according to the description given, belong to Class II. yet form their Plural as if belonging to Class III., and *vice versâ.* *In case of doubt* these two rules are fairly safe guides, and should be followed, especially as regards the more uncommon Nouns.

12. In addition to the Nouns mentioned in para. 7, the following form their Plurals irregularly :—

Singular		Plural	Singular		Plural
پلار	father.	پلاره or پلارونه	پسه	sheep.	پسونه
کال	year.	کاله or کالونه	سویه	hare.	سوئي
غل	thief.	غله	ځوئي	son.	ځامن
سل	hundred.	سوه[1] or سلګونه[2]	جِنئي	girl.	جِنکئي
شل	twenty.	شلې	سوِر	rider.	سواره
زر	thousand.	زرهِ or زرګونه[2]	پښتون	Pathan.	پُښتانه
تن	person.	تنَ	شپون	shepherd.	شپانه
کس	„	کسَ	میلمه	guest.	میلمانه
مور	mother.	میندې	راجه	raja.	راجاګان
خور	sister.	خویندې	جولا	weaver.	جولاګان
ورور	brother.	ورونړه	تارو	black partridge.	تاروګان
لور	daughter.	لونړه	مارغه	bird.	مرغان
پاو	quarter.	پاوه			

13. Some words, such as غوا a cow, ها an egg, یرغمل a hostage, have the same form in Nom. Singular and Nom. Plural.

CASE.

14. Pushtu recognizes three states of the Noun :—

1. Actor or Agent. (Nom. and Instrumental.)
2. Object. (Acc.)
3. Inflected. (Voc., Gen., Dat., Abl., Loc.)

The Nom. and Acc. have the same form in all Nouns.

The other cases have certain particles either prefixed or suffixed, or partly prefixed and partly suffixed, except the Instrumental, which has no particle.

Formation of Cases.

15. 1. The *Nominative* is the simple form of the Noun. It precedes the Accusative in all constructions with Transitive Verbs.

---

[1] Inflects to سونو.   [2] The latter forms are used only in expressions of Multitude (para 55).

2. The *Accusative* has the same form as the Nominative. It has no particle either prefixed or suffixed to it.

3. The *Vocative* is distinguished by the interjection ائي or اؤ prefixed to the Noun.

In Singular Masculine Nouns which end in a consonant the short vowel *zăwăr* (ـَ) is added to the last letter.

ائي وروړَ (Aië rōrā) O brother!

In Singular Feminine Nouns which end in a consonant the short vowel *zér* (ـِ) is added similarly.

ائي مورِ (Aië mōré) O mother!

In the Plural of ALL Nouns the interjection is prefixed to the inflected Plural form.

4. The *Genitive* is distinguished by the particle دَ (*dă*) prefixed to the Noun.

5. The *Dative* is distinguished by the particle ته or له placed after the Noun.

The former is used with reference to places, the latter with reference to persons.

6. The *Ablative* is distinguished by the particle له before the Noun, and نه after it.

When the last letter of a Noun is a consonant, the نه may be dropped, and replaced by *zăwăr*.

له كور نه or له كورَ from the house.

"*With*" (meaning "*in company with*") is rendered by دَ before the Noun and سره after it.

When "*with*" denotes an adverb of manner, it is rendered by په before the Noun, and سره after; as:—

په صلاح سره with consent. په يقين سره without any doubt, positively.

7. The *Locative* is distinguished by the particle په prefixed to the Noun. When used in conjunction with كښې suffixed it denotes "*in.*"

8. The Instrumental is simply the inflected form of the Noun without any particle. It is generally recognizable by its position at the beginning of a sentence which contains a past tense of a Transitive Verb (see paras. 25 and 110 .

Diminutives.

16. Diminutives are generally expressed by qualifying the Noun by ورُوکَي (Masc.) or ورُوکِي (Fem.), "*small.*"

A few words take the termination گیٔ to form diminutives; as—

يابو a pony.	يابوگیٔ a small pony.
مزدور a labourer.	مزدورگیٔ a small labourer.

Verbal Nouns.

17. For Verbal Nouns, see para. 70.

PRONOUNS.

18. Pronouns can be classified as :—

Personal.	Interrogative.
Demonstrative.	Correlative.
Relative.	Indefinite.
Possessive.	Pronominal Adjectives.
Reflexive.	

19. The *Personal Pronouns* are :—

زهٔ I.	مونږ we.
تهٔ thou.	تاسو or تاسي you.
هغهٔ he, she, it.	هغوئي they.

20. The Personal Pronouns are declined as follows, the cases taking their appropriate particles (para. 15), except the Genitive case, which being really the Possessive Pronoun, has no particle.

1st Person.

	SINGULAR.	PLURAL.
Nom.	زه	مونږ
Acc.	ما	مونږ
Voc.	اې زه	اې مونږ
Gen.	ځما or م	ځمونږ or مو
Dat.	ما	مونږ
Abl.	ما	مونږ
Loc.	ما	مونږ
Instr.	ما or م	مونږ

2nd Person.

	SINGULAR.	PLURAL.
Nom.	ته	تاسو
Acc.	تا	تاسو
Voc.	اې ته	اې تاسو
Gen.	ستا or دِ	ستاسو or مو
Dat.	تا	تاسو
Abl.	تا	تاسو
Loc.	تا	تاسو
Instr.	تا or دِ	تاسو

The 3rd *Person* has two forms, one referring to a Proximate and the other to a Remote object.

The Proximate (meaning "*this here*") has two forms :—

دہ when used with a Past tense of a Transitive Verb (*a*).

دې when used with an Intransitive Verb, or any tense of a Transitive Verb *other than a Past tense* (*b*).

دہ and دې are used only in the Nom. Singular. The Plural of both is دوئ used with Transitive and Intransitive Verbs.

(*a*) دہ وُوهلم He hit me.

(*b*) دې له سیند نه پوریوت He crossed the river.

دې ما وهي He is hitting me.

☛ پوریوتل "*to cross,*" is an INTRANSITIVE Verb in Pushtu.

The Remote (meaning "*that there*") is هغه. (For declension, see under Demonstrative Pronouns, para. 26.)

21. ئي, without any particle, can be used as the Genitive and the Instrumental case of both Proximate and Remote forms of the 3rd Personal Pronouns, Singular as well as Plural.

22. From para. 20 it will be noticed that in the Personal Pronouns the Accusative is among the Inflected cases, while the Vocative is not. This difference between Nouns and Pronouns should be noted.

23. The long forms of the Genitive cases, Singular and Plural, of all Personal Pronouns (really Possessive Pronouns, para. 28) are placed before the Nouns they qualify, and are frequently used to express *particularity*.

دا څما آس دئ This horse is mine.

The short forms are placed after the Nouns, and *do not necessarily* convey particularity.

آس دِ ګډ دئ Your horse is lame.

24. (1) The Personal Pronouns have also other forms in the oblique cases,—viz., را , در, ور, for 1st, 2nd and 3rd persons respectively, Singular as well as Plural. But these forms are restricted to use with the particles ته *to*, نه or نه ... له *from*, سره *with*, بانڊِ *against*, پسئ *after*; as:—

راته to me *or* us.
درنه from you.
ورسره with him *or* them.
را بانڊِ against me *or* us.
ور پسئ after him *or* them (when the sense is "*to follow*").

(2) These forms can be prefixed to Verbs to indicate the Dative; as:—

را کول to give to me *or* to us.
در ځم I am coming to you.
ورکه give him *or* them. (Colloquial form of ورکړه.)

(3) The following forms are in common use:—

ماله to me.
تاله to you.
وله to him (= ورله).

لاله (meaning "to me") is frequently met with.

ماله to me
تاله to you
دۀله to him

} are sometimes met with in books. They are never used colloquially.

پرِ meaning { on him, on her, on it *or* them }

ترِ meaning { from him, from her, from it *or* them }

} are in very common use. ☞ But note that they can be used to refer to the 3rd Person ONLY.

25. When ما, مِ, مو (1st Person); تا, دِ, مو (2nd Person), or يي (3rd Person) are used with a Transitive Verb in the Imperfect or any Past Tense, they denote the Agent.

If the long form ما, تا or مو is employed, it precedes the verb.

ما آس وشړه I drove away the horse.

If the short form مِ, دِ or يي is used, it either precedes the verb or is interposed between two parts of the verb, when the verb is divisible.

Verbs are divisible for this purpose when they prefix و in a Past tense.

آس مِ وشړه or آس و مِ شړه I drove away the horse.

26. *Demonstrative Pronouns* have two forms, the Proximate and the Remote.

The Proximate has two forms, دغه and دا, meaning "*this here.*"

دغه, when it refers to a Masculine Singular object, does not inflect in any case. When it refers to a Feminine Singular object, it inflects to دغې. The Nominative Plural is دغه (both genders); the Inflected cases Plural are دغو (both genders).

دا inflects to دې (both genders, Singular). The Nom. Plural is دا or دوي (both genders). The Inflected cases Plural have دوي (both genders).

The Remote Demonstrative Pronoun is هغه, meaning "*that there.*"

When it refers to a Masculine Singular object it remains uninflected. When it refers to a Feminine Singular object it inflects to هغې. The Nominative Plural is هغوئ for both genders. The Plural inflects to هغو.

27. *Relative Pronouns.* There is no Relative Pronoun in Pushtu. Its place is taken by the indeclinable copulative چه (that), which joins two finite sentences.

A few examples will best illustrate how the English sentence must be turned when rendering it into Pushtu.

دغه سړی دی چه لاړ	This is the man that (= who) went.
دغه جِنئ دَه چه لاړه	This is the girl that (= who) went.
دا هغه سړی دی چه نوم یئ احمد دی	This is that man that of him (= whose) the name is Ahmad.
دا هغه ونه دَه چه زه یئ لټوم	This is that tree that for it (= for which) I am searching.
دا هغه سړی دی چه زه یئ ووهلم	This is that man that by him (= by whom) I (was) struck.

28. *Possessive Pronouns.*

1st Person.	ځما	my.	ځمونږ	our.
2nd ,,	ستا	your.	ستاسو	your.
3rd ,,	یئ	his.	یئ	their.

(For position in a sentence of these Possessive Pronouns, see para. 23.)

In addition to the above is the indeclinable adjective خپل *"own,"* which when used with a Noun requires ځما, ستا etc., but when used at the beginning of a sentence refers to the subject of the Verb only.

29. *Reflexive Pronouns.* These are پخپله and ځان.

پخپله = self *or* selves. It refers to the Nominative of the sentence, and is used as an intensifying adjective. It undergoes no change for Gender or Number. It is used only in the Nominative Singular and Nominative Plural.

ځان = self *or* selves. It undergoes no change for Gender, Number, or Case. It can be used in the Nominative, or in oblique cases Singular and Plural in conjunction with the particles سره, له ... نه, په, بانْدِ. It cannot be used as the Instrumental case with Past tenses of Transitive Verbs.

ځان literally means "*body*," and is used in such expressions only as those in which the word "*body*" can be understood; *e.g.*:—

په شړۍ ځان پټ کړه Cover yourself with the blanket.

ځان پټ کړه Hide yourself.

خپل ځوئي به ځان سره راولم I will bring my son with me.

ځان is used idiomatically in such phrases as:—

ځان به اوده کړم I shall *pretend* to be asleep.

ځان ناجوړ کوي He is *pretending* to be ill.

30. *Interrogative Pronouns* are:—

(1) څوك, "*who?*" Masc. and Fem., Singular and Plur. Inflected cases چا.

څوك ئي Who are you?

چا ته واستولې Who sent you?

(2) څه, "*what?*" Indeclinable, referring to an inanimate object.

دا څه دي What is this?

(3) كوم or كُم, "*which?*" The Masculine Singular undergoes no change in the oblique cases. In the Plural it inflects to كومو or كُمو.

The Feminine Singular is formed by adding ه to the Masculine. It is then declined like a Feminine Noun of Class III. (Table A).

(4) څومره or څو "*how much?*" or "*how many?*" Indeclinable.

څو غواړي How much do you ask (want)?

څومره ملاتړ لري How many fighting men have you?

څو can be used instead of the longer form in every instance, EXCEPT in the single case in which distance is referred to.

ستاسو كلي څومره لري دي How far away is your village?

31. *Correlative Pronouns.* څومره چه "*how much that?*" followed by دومره or هومره "*so much.*"

These correlatives are used in those sentences in which "*as much as*" occurs in English.

څومره چه غواړي دومره وخوره Eat as much as you like.

څنګه چه or لِکه چه followed by هغه سيَ are *Correlatives of Manner.*

څنګه چه دِ خوښ وي هغه سيَ وکړه Do it in whichever way you like.

لِکه چه ما درته وښايل هغه سيَ وکړه Do it as I showed you.

32. *Indefinite Pronouns.*

	څوک چه	whoever. (Animate object only.)
	کوم چه	whichever. (Animate or inanimate object.)
	هرڅه چه	whatever. (Inanimate object only.)
	څوک[1]	someone, anyone.
(Inflects to هيچا)	هيڅ څوک[2] or هيڅوک	no one, nobody.
(Indeclinable)	څه[1]	something, anything.
(Inflects to بعضو)	بعضيَ[1]	some people.
(,, ځنو)	ځنيَ[1]	some people.
(Indeclinable)	هيڅ . . . نه	no one, nothing.

Fem.	Masc.	
	يو	one (used impersonally).
بله	بل	another.
بله يوه	بل يو	another one.
کومه يوه	کوم يو	which one ?
هره يوه	هر يو	every one.
نوريَ تولي	نور تول	all the rest.
نوريَ ديريَ	نور دير	many more, many another.
بله څوک	بل څوک	another person.
نوريَ څوک	نور څوک	who else ?
	بل څه	another thing.
	نور څه	what else ?
	هر څوک	everybody.
	هر څه	everything.
	هر څو	however many.

---

[1] Can be converted from Positive to Negative by the addition of the Negative Particle نه to a Verb.

[2] When followed by the Negative Particle نه the negative is intensified.

33. *Pronominal Adjectives.* دواړه both.

(Fem.) ډېره (Masc.) ډېر much. *In plural,* many.

نوره نور more.

هره هر every.

توَل } all.
واړه }

يو څو a few.

ADJECTIVES.

34. When an Adjective qualifies a Noun it precedes it, as in English.

ښه سړی A good man.

When an Adjective follows a Noun it is the complement of the sentence.

سړی ښه دی The man is good.

35. An Adjective agrees in Gender, Number, and Case with the Noun which it qualifies.

When an Adjective qualifies two or more Nouns of different genders, it is repeated for each Noun.

دَ کلِي زاړه سړي او زړی ښځی په منَ راغلی[1] The old men and women of the village met us.

☛ [1] راغلي, being in the 3rd person agrees in Gender as well as in Number and Person with the Noun NEAREST TO IT IN THE SENTENCE.

36. The majority of Adjectives ending in a consonant remain unchanged in the Nominative Plural Masculine.

They form the Feminine Singular by adding ه to the Masculine Singular, and are then declined like Feminine Nouns of Class III. (Table A).

Feminine. Plural.	Feminine. Singular.	Masculine. Singular and Plural.	
یخې	یخه	یخ	cold.
محکمې	محکمه	محکم	steady, firm.
حاجتمندې	حاجتمنده	حاجتمند	poor.
وچې	وچه	وچ	dry.

37. The following Adjectives, however, are quite irregular in the way they form the Masculine Plural and Feminine Singular :—

Feminine. Plural.	Feminine. Singular.	Masculine. Plural.	Masculine. Singular.	
پرتې	پرته	پراته	پروت	lying down.
پخې	پخه	پاخه	پوخ	ripe.
پستې	پسته	پاسته	پوست	soft.
ترخې	ترخه	تارخه	تریخ	bitter.
تروې	تروه	تاروه	تریو	sour.
تودې	توده	تاوده	تود	hot.
څربې	څربه	څاربه	څورب	fat.
خورې	خوره	خواره	خور	scattered.
خوږې	خوږه	خواږه	خوږ	sweet.
درنې	درنه	درانه	دروند	heavy.
رڼې	رڼه	راڼه	روڼ	bright.
ړندې	ړنده	ړانده	ړوند	blind.
زړې	زړه	زاړه	زوړ	old.
سورې	سوره	سواره	سور	riding (a rider).
سړې	سړه	ساړه	سوړ	cold.
کږې	کږه	کاږه	کوږ	crooked.
کڼې	کڼه	کاڼه	کوڼ	deaf.
لوندې	لونده	لاونده	لوند	wet.
مړې	مړه	ماړه	موړ	rich, satisfied.

All the above drop the in the inflected cases Masculine Plural, as :—

دَ ړندو سړو of blind men.

په خورو کورونو کښې in the scattered houses.

Also these Adjectives are irregular :—

Feminine.		Masculine.		
PLURAL.	SINGULAR.	PLURAL.	SINGULAR.	
سرَي	سرَه	سره	سور	red.
مړَي	مړَه	مړه	مړ	dead.
شنَي	شنه	شنه	شين	green, bright, clear (of the sky).
غونډَي	غونډه	غونډي	غونډ	spherical.
نورَي	بله	نور	بل	other.

38. Adjectives ending in ه have the same form for the Nominative cases Masculine Singular and Plural and Feminine Singular.

The oblique cases Masculine Singular do not inflect.

The oblique cases Masculine Plural inflect to و.

The Feminine follows the rule for Feminine Nouns of Class III. (Table A).

ښه سړَي a good man.
ښه سړي good men.
ښه ښځه a good woman.
ښې ښځې good women.
دَ ښه سړي of a good man.
دَ ښو سړو of good men.
دَ ښې ښځې of a good woman.
دَ ښو ښځو of good women.

The Exceptions are :—

(1) خپه sorry.

(2) پوه[1] well-informed.

Both of these remain unchanged in the Nominative cases Singular and Plural (Masculine and Feminine).

(1) خپه in the oblique cases Masculine and Feminine Singular does not inflect.

The oblique cases Masculine and Feminine Plural inflect to و.

---

[1] Colloquially پوَي.

(2) [1]پوره The Masculine Singular does not inflect in oblique cases.
The Masculine Plural ADDS و ([2]پورهو).
The Feminine follows the rule for Feminine Nouns of Class III. (Table A) for the formation of oblique cases Sing. and Plural.

39. Adjectives in ي form their Masculine Plural, Feminine Singular, and Feminine Plural in different ways, as :—

Feminine.		Masculine.		
Plural.	Singular.	Plural.	Singular.	
پاسنئي		پاسنِي	پاسنَي	upper.
ښکتنئي		ښکتنِي	ښکتنَي	lower.
ښئي		ښِي	ښَي	right (opp. to "left")
ګړندئي		ګړندِي	ګړندَي	swift.
مندرئي		مندرِي	مندرَي	short.
نرئي		نرِي	نرَي	thin.
لويئي	لويه	لوئي		great.
تږَي		تږِي	تږَي	thirsty.
ورکوټَي		ورکوټِي	ورکوټَي	small.
وړوکَي		وړوکِي	وړوکَي	small.
وږَي		وږَي	وږَي	hungry.

40. Adjectives can be formed from Proper Nouns by the addition of وال or ي when the termination denotes "*an inhabitant of,*" as :—

بنيروال an inhabitant of Buner.
قندهاري „ Kandahar.
پيښاوري „ Peshawar.

وال can also be added to an ordinary Noun in the same way.
کليوال a villager, from کلي a village.

"An inhabitant of" can also be expressed by the Genitive case, as :—
دَ کابل سړَي a man from Kabul = a Kabuli.

---

[1] Colloquially پوئي.

[2] Colloquially پويو.

The Genitive case is also used with Proper Nouns in such expressions as "*the Kabul River,*" where in English the word "Kabul" is used as an Adjective.

دَ کابل سیند the Kabul River.

دَ افغانستان غرونه the Afghan Mountains.

41. Adjectives can also be formed from Adverbs by adding ي or ني to the Adverb, thus :—

پروني	yesterday's,	from	پرون
ښکتني	lower,	,,	ښکته
لاندني	lower,	,,	لاندِ
ورستني	last,	,,	ورستو

Comparison of Adjectives.

42. As in Urdu, so in Pushtu, Adjectives have no Degrees of Comparison, and the same roundabout method of expressing the Comparative and Superlative Degrees must be employed.

43. *The Comparative Degree.* The object with which the subject of the sentence is compared is put into the Ablative case, the Adjective agreeing with the subject in Gender and Number ; e.g. :—

هلک له جنئ نه مشر دئ The boy is older than the girl.

(Literally, "The boy from the girl is old," the Adjective being Masculine Singular, agreeing with "boy.")

جِنکئ له هلکانو نه مشرئ دي The girls are older than the boys.

(Literally, "The girls from the boys are old," the Adjective being Feminine Plural, agreeing with "girls.")

44. *The Superlative Degree.* A similar method to the above is employed, except that the subject of the sentence is compared with *all others of its kind ;* the Adjective, as before, agreeing with the subject in Gender and Number ; e.g. :—

دغه سړئ له تولو نه مضبوط دئ This man is the strongest.

(Literally, "This man from all is strong.")

دغه ښځئ له تولو نه مړئ دي These are the richest women.

(Literally, "These women from all are rich.")

VERBAL ADJECTIVES.

45. The following Verbal Adjectives, when qualifying Masculine Nouns, are declined like Nouns of Class II., Table B; when qualifying Feminine Nouns, they add ه, and are then declined like Nouns of Class III., Table A.

روان	moving.	ناست	sitting.
لاړ	went, gone.	ولاړ	standing.
ملاست	lying down.	هیسار	stopped, waiting.

ABSTRACT NOUNS.

46. Abstract Nouns are words denoting Qualities or Actions. They can be formed from Nouns or Adjectives in various ways.

میلمستیا	hospitality,	from	میلمه	a guest.
زړهورتوب or زړهورتیا	bravery,	„	زړهور	brave.
ناجوړتیا	sickness,	„	ناجوړ	sick.
هلکوالي or هلکتیا	boyhood,	„	هلک	a boy.
سموالي	straightness,	„	سم	straight.

NUMERALS.

47. The Fractions are :—

پاو	¼	یو نیم	1½
نیم	½	پاو کم دوه	1¾
درې پاوه	¾	پاو باندې دوه	2¼
پنځه پاوه	1¼	دوه نیم	2½

and so on.

پاو (plural پاوه), *a quarter,* when used with another number, precedes it.

نیم, *a half,* when joined to another number, follows it.

48. The Cardinal Numbers are :—

١	(Fem. يوه) يو	1	١٩	نولس	19
٢	دوه	2	٢٠	شل	20
٣	درې	3	٢١	يو ويشت	21
٤	څلور	4	٢٢	دوه ويشت	22
٥	پنځه	5	٣٠	ديرش	30
٦	شپږ	6	٤٠	څلويښت	40
٧	اوه	7	٥٠	پنځوس	50
٨	اته	8	٦٠	شپيته	60
٩	نهه	9	٧٠	اويا	70
١٠	لس	10	٨٠	اتيا	80
١١	يولس	11	٩٠	نوي	90
١٢	دولس	12	١٠٠	سل	100
١٣	ديارلس	13		or لس دَ پاسَ سل	110
١٤	سوارلس	14	١١٠	لس باندِ سل	
١٥	پنځلس	15	٢٠٠	دوه سوه	200
١٦	شپاړس	16	١٠٠٠	زر	1000
١٧	اوه لس	17	١٠٠٠٠٠	لک	100,000
١٨	اتلس	18			

49. Although the intermediate numbers over 20 can be given as shown above, yet the following forms are also common :—

1 more than 20	يو دَ پاسَ شل or يو باندِ شل	21
2 ,, ,, ,,	دوه دَ پاسَ شل or دوه باندِ شل	22
4 ,, ,, 30	څلور دَ پاسَ ديرش or څلور باندِ ديرش	34
1 less than 40	يو کم څلويښت	39

50. Among uneducated Pathans counting above 39 is carried on by "scores" شلې (plur. of شل, 20), thus :—

2 twenties	=	دوه شلې	40
2½ ,,	=	دوه نيمې شلې	50
3 ,,	=	درې شلې	60

3½	twenties	=	دريَ نيميَ شلـيَ	70
4	,,	=	څلور شلـيَ	80
4½	,,	=	څلور نيميَ شلـيَ	90
5	,,	=	پِنځه شلـيَ	100
5½	,,	=	پِنځه نيميَ شلـيَ	110
6	,,	=	شپږ شلـيَ	120

etc., etc.

Under this system, *which is the commonest method, even among educated Pathans,* the intermediate numbers are :—

1 more than 2 score	يو دَ پاسَ (or يو باندِ) دوه شلـيَ	41
5 ,, ,, 2½ ,,	پِنځه دَ پاسَ (or پِنځه باندِ) دوه نيميَ شلـيَ	55
3 ,, ,, 4½ ,,	دريَ دَ پاسَ (or دريَ باندِ) څلور نيميَ شلـيَ	93
8 ,, ,, 5 ,,	اته دَ پاسَ (or اته باندِ) پِنځه شلـيَ	108

and so on.

51. يو, *one,* is the only Cardinal Number which has a Feminine Form (يَوه).
The Masculine remains uninflected in all cases.
The Feminine inflects to يوئَ.

The other Cardinal numbers inflect thus :—

دوه و	اوه و
دريو	اتو
څلورو	نهو
پِنځو	لسو
شپږو	يولسو etc.

52. *"About."* To express an approximate number the word يو is placed before the number, if it is ten or less. If the number is more than ten the word قريب, *"about,"* is used.

يو پِنځه سړي about five men.

قريب شل سړي about twenty men.

53. *Distribution* is expressed by repeating the Cardinal Number.

یو یو one by one.

دوه دوه two by two.

پنځه پنځه سړي را دِ شي Let five men come at a time.

54. *Multiplication* is expressed by help of the particle په with یو.

یو په دوه twice as much.

یو په درې three times as much.

55. *Multitude* is expressed by using the particle په with the inflected plural forms of the Cardinal Numbers.

په لسو by tens.

په سلګونو by hundreds.

په زرګونو by thousands.

56. *Universality* is denoted by واړه, *"all,"* placed after the Cardinal Number.

دواړه (= دوه واړه) both.

څلور واړه all four.

لس واړه all ten.

ORDINAL NUMBERS.

57. *"First"* is وړندې (Fem. وړندۍ). The Persian form اول (Fem. اوله) is also used.

"Second" is دویم, from دوه, *"two."* All other Cardinal Numbers ending in ه change that letter to م to form the corresponding Ordinal Numbers, as :—

اتم 8th, from اته 8.

نهم 9th, ,, نه 9.

Cardinal Numbers which end in ا or ي add یم, as :—

دریيم 3rd, from درې 3.

اتيایم 80th, ,, اتيا 80.

The other Cardinal Numbers add م to form their Ordinals, as :—

لسم 10th, from لس 10.
پنځوسم 50th, „ پنځوس 50.

The Feminine is formed by adding ه to the final م.

58. *Formation of Plural.* The Nominative Singular and Nominative Plural are alike.

The Feminine Ordinals follow the rule for Feminine Nouns of Class III., Table A.

59. *Formation of Cases.* In Masculine Ordinals the oblique cases Singular and Plural undergo no change.

The Feminine Ordinals follow the rule for Feminine Nouns of Class III., Table A.

CHAPTER II.

VERBS.

60. Pushtu Verbs end in one of three ways :—

(1) ل preceded by a consonant. Such Verbs are either Transitive or Intransitive.

(2) ول. Such Verbs are all Transitive, being Derivatives of کول, "*to do.*"

(3) یدل. Such Verbs are either "Original" Verbs, in which case they can be either Transitive or Intransitive, or they are Derivatives of کیدل, "*to become,*" and are Intransitive.

61. Transitive Verbs have an Active and a Passive form.

In translating English into Pushtu, never use a Verb in the Passive form if, by turning the sentence, the Active form can be employed.

62. *Derivative Verbs* are those formed by conjugating a Noun, Adverb, or Adjective with either of the Auxiliary Verbs کیدل or کول.

Similarly a Passive Verb is a Past Participle conjugated with کیدل, "*to become.*" The Past Participle is treated as a Noun (see para. 64).

63. These Compound Verbs have many peculiarities which must be carefully noted. Attention is drawn to them on pages 48 to 51, where examples of such Verbs are given.

64. It will not be necessary to give examples of کیدل and کول conjugated with a Noun or Adverb if the following points are borne in mind :—

کيدل *with Noun or Adverb.* These compounds follow the same rules as compounds of کيدل with Adjectives (pages 48 and 49), except that in Column 1A the و of the parent verb is retained.

کول *with Noun.* No union takes place between Noun and Verb. Both are declined independently.

کول *with Adverb.* No union takes place between Adverb and Verb, BUT the و in Column 1A is dropped.

65. When either of the Auxiliary Verbs is compounded with an Adjective, the کښ of the Verb can only be dropped when the Adjective ends in a consonant and adds ه for the Feminine Singular; for it is from the Feminine Singular of the Adjective that such Verbs are formed. The final ه of the Adjective and the initial کښ of the Verb are then both elided, and the two words run into one :—

Examples :—

COMPOUND WITH کول	COMPOUND WITH کيدل	FEMININE SINGULAR.	ADJECTIVE.
ګرمَول	ګرميدل	ګرمه	ګرم warm.
پخَول	پخيدل	پخه	پوخ ripe.
ترخَول	ترخيدل	ترخه	تريخ bitter.

It must also be noted that when an Adjective thus combines with کول the sound of the ه is not lost, but the Adjective takes the short vowel *zawar* in the Infinitive and in Columns 1, 2, 3, and 5 (*vide* Note (1), page 51).

66. If an Adjective ends in a long vowel, or aspirated ه, no union takes place. The Adjective and Verb are placed side by side, and the Verb conjugated independently.

67. Nouns expressing rank or dignity, *e.g.* King, Raja, Subadar, etc., when used in connection with these Verbs are regarded as Adjectives, BUT ONLY in Columns 1A and 4.

68. In the Compound Verbs—

راكول to give to me *or* us,
دركول ,, ,, you,
وركول ,, ,, him *or* them,

the prefixed و of the parent Verb is dropped. In other respects the parent Verb undergoes no change.

MOODS.

69. The Pushtu Verb has seven Moods :—

Infinitive.
Indicative.
Imperative.
Subjunctive.
Conditional.
Optative.
Potential.

70. *The Infinitive* is the simple form of the Verb. It is frequently used as a Verbal Noun, in which case it is treated as a plural word, requires a plural Verb, and inflects by adding و.

A contracted form of the inflected cases (of the Verbal Noun) is very common, ليدو for ليدلو ; اخستو for اخستلو etc., etc.

The Infinitive Mood comprises :—

The Verbal Noun.
The Active Agent.
The Gerund.
The Past Participle.

71. *The Indicative Mood* has eight tenses :—

Present.
Future, *two* (weak and strong).
Imperfect.
Habitual Imperfect.
Perfect.
Aorist. (Simple Past.)
Pluperfect.

72. *The Imperative Mood* has two forms, the Continuous and the Definite.

Strictly speaking, the Imperative Mood has only two persons, the 2nd Singular and the 2nd Plural; but the 1st and 3rd persons, under the forms "Let me or us" and "Let him or them," have also been included in this Mood.

For the 1st Person (Singular or Plural) the idiom is ځه چه, introducing a finite verb; ځه itself being the 2nd Singular (continuous) Imperative of تلل, "*to go.*" The particle چه requires that the following verb should be in the Subjunctive Mood.

Examples:—

ځه چه راشو Let us come; literally, "Go! that we may come."

ځه چه ووايو Let us say; " "Go! that we may say."

But—ځه چه ځو Let us go; where ځو is Indicative, not Subjunctive.

The 2nd Persons (Singular and Plural) are certain inflected forms of the Verb. The rule for forming them is given in Table C.

The 3rd Person (Singular and Plural) is rendered by inserting the particle دِ between the personal pronoun and the 3rd Person Present Indicative or Present Subjunctive. E.g.:—

هغه دِ ځي or هغه دِ لاړ شي Let him go.

هغوئ دِ ځي or هغوئ دِ لاړ شي Let them go.

NOTE the difference between:—

دِ with a Verb. | دِ with a Noun.

The former precedes the Verb, and means "LET." The latter follows the Noun, and means "YOUR."

73. *The Subjunctive Mood* has three tenses:—

Present. Past. Doubtful Past.

74. *The Conditional Mood* has only one tense peculiar to itself—the Pluperfect.

Conditional sentences are introduced by كه "*if*," كله "*when*," etc., which particles require the Subjunctive Mood. Therefore tenses of the Subjunctive Mood may be said to be tenses of the Conditional Mood; but whether Subjunctive or Conditional, they are the same in form.

75. The Pluperfect Conditional is unique in that the Verb is used impersonally in the 3rd singular, the subject of the English sentence being a Noun or Personal Pronoun. E.g. :—

راغلي وي	زه ته هغه etc.	که	If	I you he etc.	had come.

The form راغلي وي *never changes,* no matter what the subject of the English sentence may be, whether Masculine, Feminine, Singular or Plural, or what Person.

76. Conditional sentences consist of two parts ; the first introduced by "if," "when," etc., and the second joined by the conjunction "then." This conjunction is frequently omitted in English, *but must always be expressed in Pushtu.*

Examples :—

که زه راغلي وي نو ليدلي به دِ وم — If I had come (then) you would have seen me.

که زه حاضر نه وي نو بيشکښ لويدلي به وي — If I had not been present (then) you certainly would have fallen.

77. *The Optative Mood* (see para. 123).

78. *The Potential Mood* has three tenses :—

Present. Future. Past.

79. *Formation of Tenses,* etc., of the various Moods.—These are shown in Table C, which must be committed to memory. The columns should be read vertically.

See Preface for an explanation of this Table.

When conversing with Pathans remember that they always add the short vowel *zawar* to the first person singular of all tenses.

80. TABLE C. **INFINITIVE,**

1 — **1A** — **2**

Pres. Indicative.	Pres. Subjunctive.	Verbal Noun.
Change final ل of the Infin. to م, تړم	Prefix و to Pres. Indic., وتړم	Same as Infin., تړل

Future.

Weak.	Strong.	Active Agent.
Prefix به to Pres. Indic., به تړم	Prefix به to Pres. Subjunc., به وتړم	Final ل of Infin. becomes: ونکي for mas., تړونکي ونکې for fem., تړونکې

Imperative.

Continuous.	Definite.	Gerund.
Change final م of Pres. Indic. to: ه for 2nd Sing., تړه ئ for 2nd Pl., تړئ	Change final م of Pres. Subjunc. to: ه for 2nd Sing., وتړه ئ for 2nd Pl., وتړئ	Final ل of Infin. becomes: ون for mas., تړون نه for fem., تړنه

Notes.

(1) The masculine form of the Gerund is seldom used. The Gerund is declined like an ordinary Noun.

(2) Verbs which form their Pres. Indic. and Pres. Subjunc. regularly according to the above rules have only the 1st form in Col. 3. They cannot have the 2nd form, because if it existed it would be exactly like one of the other tenses of the verb, i.e. either Pres. Indic., Pres. Subj., or Aorist.

تړل, *to bind*, cannot have the 2nd form, for it would then be the same as the Pres. Indic., تړم

راوړل, *to bring*, cannot have the 2nd form, for it would then be the same as the Pres. Subj., راوړم

استول, *to send*, cannot have the 2nd form (in the Aor.), for it would then be the same as the Pres. Subj., واستوم

تړل "to bind."

3

Imperf. Indicative.
1st Form:
Add م to Infin.,
تړلم
2nd Form:
Change final ل of Infin. to م
(*See Note 2 below.*)

Habitual Imperf.
Prefix به to the 2 forms of Imperf. Indic. (if the verb has both forms),
به تړلم

Aorist.
Prefix و to Imperf. Indic.,
وتړلم

4

Past Participle.
Add ي to Infin.,
تړلي

Perfect Indicative.
Add يم to Past Participle,
تړلي يم

Pluperf. Conditional.
Add وي to Past Participle,
تړلي وي

Doubtful Past.
Prefix به to Perf. Indic.,
تړلي به يم

Pluperf. Indicative.
Add وم to Past Participle,
تړلي وم

Past Subjunctive.
Prefix به to Pluperf. Indic.,
تړلي به وم

Present Potential.
Add شم to Past Participle,
تړلي شم

Future Potential.
Prefix به to Pres. Potential,
تړلي به شم

Past Potential.
Add شوم to Past Participle,
تړلي شوم

Notes (*continued*).

(3) The 3rd plur. masc. Imperf. Indic. is exactly like the Infin. in form.

(4) څملاستل, *to lie down*, کښيناستل, *to sit down*, ننوتل, *to enter*, and verbs beginning with پ - را - کي do not prefix و in any tense. The following verbs are exceptions to this rule:—

پړخيدل *to swell*	پوهيدل *to know*	پښتيدل *to ask*
پرزيدل *to be knocked down*	پيژندل *to recognise*	

(5) Verbs whose Infinitives end in ول, drop a و when forming the Active Agent.

81. In all tenses of Intransitive Verbs, as well as in Present and Future tenses of Transitive Verbs, the different persons Singular and Plural are distinguished by certain suffixes which form part of the verb, and serve to indicate the Subject.

These terminations are :—

	SINGULAR.	PLURAL.
1st Person	ـه	و
2nd ,,	ې	ئ
3rd ,,	etc. ي, ه, ل, ت	ي, ل, ت

Many tenses have Masculine and Feminine forms for the 3rd persons Singular and Plural.

The Present Indicative of کيدل is conjugated out in full on p. 40. It will illustrate this paragraph, and serve to show how all tenses of other verbs are conjugated.

In the following pages, therefore, the 1st Singular of each tense is given, except where the whole tense is irregular, or where one or more persons are irregularly formed. In such cases, either the whole tense is conjugated, or merely the irregular form stated, as well as the 1st Person Singular.

82. The suffixes mentioned in the preceding paragraph alone sufficiently denote the person or subject of the sentence, hence the addition of personal pronouns is generally unnecessary.

When used they are :—

	SINGULAR.	PLURAL.
1st Person	زه	مونږ
2nd ,,	ته	تاسو
3rd ,,	هغه	هغوئ

83. Verbs whose Infinitives end in يدل change the د into ږ before forming the Present Indicative. Such verbs are conjugated like لويدل (pages 54 and 55).

84. The following Verbs are exceptions to the above rule :—

PRESENT INDICATIVE.	INFINITIVE.	
اورم	اوريدل	to hear.
اوړم	اوړيدل	to climb over.
اوسم	اوسيدل	to live, dwell.

PRESENT INDICATIVE.	INFINITIVE.	
بریخم	بریخیدل	to flash, glitter.
پاخم	پاخیدل[1]	to arise, get up.
تښتم	تښتیدل	to run away, flee.
څرم	څریدل	to graze.
رسم	رسیدل	to arrive, reach.
رغړم	رغړیدل	to roll, roll down.
زغلم	زغلیدل	to run (a race).
ګرزم	ګرزیدل	to walk, wander.
وینم / ګورم	لیدل	to see.

85. Verbs whose Infinitives end in تل change the ت into ز or ږ before forming the Present Indicative.

86. The following Verbs are exceptions to the above rule :—

PRES. SUBJ.	PRESENT INDIC.	INFINITIVE.	
	اخلم	اخستل[2]	to take *or* buy.
	آغوندم	آغوستل	to wear.
بوزم	بیایم	بوتلل	to take away (of animate objects).
	پوریباسم	پوریستل	to cause to cross.
	پریباسم	پریستل[1]	to knock down.
	تیرباسم	تیریستل	to mislead.
څملم	څملم	څملاستل[1]	to lie down.
	خیژم	ختل	to climb, rise (of the sun).
	راولم	راوستل[1]	to bring.
	ساتم	ساتل	to keep.
	غوارم	غوښتل	to ask, want.

---

[1] See Note (4), Table C. [2] Past Participle اخستلی or اخستی

Pres. Subj.	Present Indic.	Infinitive.	
	کښېنم	کښېناستل[1]	to sit.
	لولم	لوستل	to read.
	لونم	لوستل	to scatter seed.
	نښلم	نښتل	to cling to.
	نغاړم	نغښتل	to roll up.
وباسم	وباسم	ويستل	to take out, draw (sword), take off clothes.
	ولم	ويشتل	to throw, shoot.

87. The Verbs in para. 84, together with the following, are Original Infinitives :—

بهيدل	to flow.	شليدل	to tear.
پړسيدل	to swell.	غړيدل	to slip away.
پرزيدل	to be knocked down.	کړيدل	to live in pain, be tortured.
پوهيدل	to know.		
څڅيدل	to leak.	ګړزيدل	to thunder.
جنګيدل	to strike against.	لړزيدل	to tremble.
چليدل	to travel backwards and forwards.	لګيدل	to reach, hit.
		لويدل	to fall.
خوځيدل	to shake, move.	ليګديدل	to be loaded.
خويدل	to slip.	نړيدل	to fall down.
رپيدل	to shiver.	ودريدل	to stand, wait.
ړچيدل	to shake, be rickety.	وريدل	to rain, snow.

88. Causal Verbs can be formed from all Original Infinitives by changing يدل of the latter into ول.

لويدل, *to fall*, and ليدل, *to see*, have no causal forms.

---

[1] See Note (4), Table C.

89. THE DEFECTIVE AUXILIARY VERB TO BE.

PRESENT (DEFINITE).

زه يم I am.
ته يئ thou art.
هغه دي he is.
هغه ده she is.
مونږ يو we are.
تاسو يئ you are.
هغوئ دي they are.

PRESENT (CONTINUOUS).

This tense is exactly like the Present Definite, except that the

3rd Singular is هغه وي for both genders.
3rd Plural is هغوئ وي „ „

FUTURE (WEAK).

زه به يم I will be.
ته به يئ thou wilt be.
هغه به وي he, she, it will be.
مونږ به يو we will be.
تاسو به يئ you will be.
هغوئ به وي they will be.

FUTURE (STRONG).

زه به شم I shall be.
ته به شې thou shalt be.
هغه به شي he, she, it shall be.
مونږ به شو we shall be.
تاسو به شئ you shall be.
هغوئ به شي they shall be.

AORIST (SIMPLE PAST).

زه وم I was.
ته وې thou wast.
هغه وُه he was.
هغه وَه she was.
مونږ وُو we were.
تاسو وئ you were.
هغوئ وُو they (mas.) were.
هغوئ وې they (fem.) were.

PAST SUBJUNCTIVE.

زه به وم I might *or* would have been.

(Conjugated throughout like the Aorist.)

90. کیدل To Become.

1

Pres. Indicative.
(I become.)

زه کیږم
ته کیږې
هغه کیږي
مونږ کیږو
تاسو کیږئ
هغوئ کیږي

Future.

Weak.
(I will become.)

زه به کیږم
etc.

Continuous.

ته کیږه
تاسو کیږئ

Imperative.

become thou.
become ye.

1a

Pres. Subjunc.
(I may become.)

زه وشم
etc.
(conjugated like the Strong Future in para. .)

Strong.
(I shall become.)

زه به وشم
etc.

Definite.

ته وشه
تاسو وشئ

Aorist.
(I became.)

1st Form.	2nd Form.
زه وشولم	زه وشوم
ته وشولې	ته وشوې
هغه وشوله (f.)	هغه وشه (m.) / وشوه (f.)
مونږ وشولو	مونږ وشو
تاسو وشولئ	تاسو وشوئ
هغوې وشولې (f.)	هغوئ وشول / وشو (m.); وشوې (f.)

2

Verbal Noun.
(the becoming.)

کیدل

Active Agent.

کیدونکی he who becomes.

کیدونکې she who becomes.

Gerund.
(a becoming.)

کیدنه

Notes.

The peculiarities of this Verb are :—

(1) The tenses of Columns 1a and 4 are formed from a non-existent Infinitive شول.

(2) The Aorist belongs to Column 1a, and not to Column 3.

(3) The Potential Mood (Column 5) is formed, not from the actual Past Participle, but from what one would have expected the Past Participle to be.

Irregular Auxiliary Intransitive Verb.

3

Imperfect Indicative.
(I was becoming.)

1st Form.	*2nd Form.*
زۀ کيدلم	زۀ کيدم
تۀ کيدلې	تۀ کيدې
هغه کيدله (*f.*)	هغه کيدۀ (*m.*)
مونږ کيدلو	مونږ کيدو
تاسو کيدلئ	تاسو کيدئ
هغوئ کيدلې (*f.*)	هغوئ کيدل (*m.*)

Habitual Imperfect.
(I used to become, *or* I was in the habit of becoming.)

1st Form.	*2nd Form.*
زۀ به کيدلم	زۀ به کيدم

etc.

4

Past Participle.
(having become.)
شوې

Perfect Indicative.
(I have become.)
زۀ شوې يم
etc.
مونږ شوي يو
etc.

Pluperf. Condit.
(If I had become.)
کۀ زۀ شوې وې

Doubtful Past.
(I may have become.)
زۀ شوې به يم
etc.

Pluperf. Indicative.
(I had become.)
زۀ شوې وم
etc.

Past Subjunctive.
(I might *or* would have become.)
زۀ شوې به وم
etc.

5

Present Potential
(I can become.)
زۀ کيدلې شم
etc.

Future Potential.
(I shall be able to become.)
زۀ کيدلې به شم
etc.

Past Potential.
(I could become.)
زۀ کيدلې شوم
etc.

N.B. The *colloquial* form of tenses of this Column is:—
زۀ کيدې شم

91. کول To Do *or* Make.

1

1A

Pres. Indicative.
(I do.)
زه کوم
etc.

Pres. Subjunct.
(I may do.)
زه وکړم
ته وکړې
وکړي
وکا or کا } دغه
وکاندِ or کاندِ
etc.

Future.

Weak.
(I will do.)
زه به کوم
etc.

Strong.
(I shall do.)
زه به وکړم
etc.

Imperative.

Continuous.
ته کوه — do thou.
تاسو کوئ — do ye.

Definite.
ته وکړه — do thou.
تاسو وکړئ — do ye.

Aorist.
وکړلم
وکړلې
وکړ (*m.*) }
وکړله (*f.*) }
وکړلو
وکړلئ
وکړل (*m.*) }
وکړلې (*f.*) }

2

Verbal Noun.
(the doing.)
کول

Active Agent.
کونکې he who does.
کونکي she who does.

Gerund.
(a doing.)
کونه

IRREGULAR AUXILIARY TRANSITIVE VERB.

3

IMPERF. INDICATIVE.

کولم

کولې

(*m.*) کوه

(*m.*) کاوه

(*f.*) کوله

کولو

کولئ

(*m.*) کول

(*f.*) کولې

HABITUAL IMPERFECT.

به کولم

etc.

4

PAST PARTICIPLE.
(having done.)

کړې

PERFECT INDICATIVE.

کړي یم

etc.

PLUPERF. CONDITIONAL.
(If I had done.)

که ما کړې وې

DOUBTFUL PAST.

کړې به یم

etc.

PLUPERF. INDICATIVE.

کړې وم

etc.

PAST SUBJUNCTIVE.

کړې به وم

etc.

5

PRESENT POTENTIAL.
(I can do.)

زه کولې شم

etc.

FUTURE POTENTIAL.
(I shall be able to do.)

زه کولې به شم

etc.

PAST POTENTIAL.

کولې شوم

etc.

NOTES.

The peculiarities of this Verb are :—

(1) The tenses of Columns 1A and 4 are derived from a non-existent Infinitive کړل.

(2) The Aorist belongs to Column 1A, and not to Column 3.

(3) The Potential Mood is formed from what we should have expected the Past Participle to be.

92. تلل

1 — **1A** — **2**

1. Pres. Indic. (I go.)
زه ځم
etc.

Future.

Weak. (I will go.)
زه به ځم
etc.

Imperative.

Continuous.

ته ځه	go thou.
تاسو ځئي	go ye.
هغه } دِ ځي	let him go.
هغوئي } دِ ځي	let them go.

1A. Pres. Subjunctive. (I may go.)
زه لاړ شم
etc.

Strong. (I shall go.)
زه به لاړ شم
etc.

Definite.
ته لاړ شه
تاسو لاړ شئي
هغه } دِ لاړ شي
هغوئي } دِ لاړ شي

Aorist. (I went.)
زه لاړم
ته لاړې
هغه } لاړ (*m.*)
هغه } لاړه، لاړله (*f.*)
etc.
هغوئي } لاړل (*m.*)
هغوئي } لاړې (*f.*).

2. Verbal Noun. (the going.)
تلل

Active Agent.
تلونکی he who goes.
تلونکې she who goes.

Gerund. (a going.)
تلنه

Notes.

تلل has the following peculiarities:—

(1) The Present Subjunctive is not formed from the Present Indicative, which itself is irregular.

(2) The Aorist is formed from the Present Subjunctive.

(3) The Khattacks and Afridis use لاړ for تلې all through Column 4, except in the Potential Mood.

To Go.

3

Imperfect Indicative.
(I was going.)

1st Form.	*2nd Form.*
زه تللم[1]	زه تلم
ته تللې	ته تلې
هغه { تلو (*m.*) / تلله (*f.*) }	هغه { تۀ (*m.*) / تله (*f.*) }
مونږ تللو	مونږ تلو
تاسو تللئ	تاسو تلئ
هغوئ { تلل (*m.*) / تللې (*f.*) }	هغوئ { تلل (*m.*) / تلې (*f.*) }

Habitual Imperfect.
(I used to go,
or I was in the habit of going.)

1st Form.	*2nd Form.*
زه به تللم[1]	زه به تلم

etc.

4

Past Participle.
(Having gone.)
تلې[2]

Perfect Indicative.
(I have gone.)
زه تلې يم
etc.

Pluperfect Conditional.
(If I had gone.)
که زه تلې وې

Doubtful Past.
(I may have gone.)
زه تلې به يم
etc.

Pluperfect Indicative.
(I had gone.)
زه تلې وم
etc.

Past Subjunctive.
(I might *or* would have gone.)
زه تلې به وم
etc.

Present Potential.
(I can go.)
زه تلې شم
etc.

Future Potential.
(I shall be able to go.)
زه تلې به شم
etc.

Past Potential.
(I could go.)
زه تلې شوم
etc.

---

[1] Not often used.

[2] The regularly formed Past Participle تللی does exist, but it is not frequently used. It is reserved for the Past Participle of تلل, "to weigh."

93. راتلل

1		1A	2
Present Indic. (I come.) زه راځم etc.		**Present Subj.** (I may come.) زه راشم etc.	**Verbal Noun.** (the coming.) راتلل
Weak. (I will come.) زه به راځم etc.	**Future.**	**Strong.** (I shall come.) زه به راشم etc.	
Continuous.	**Imperative.**	**Definite.**	**Active Agent.**
ته راځه	come thou.	ته راشه	راتلونكي he who comes.
تاسو راځئ	come ye.	تاسو راشئ	راتلونكي she who comes.
هغه } دِ راځي	let him come.	هغه } دِ راشي	**Gerund.** (a coming.)
هغوئ } دِ راځي	let them come.	هغوئ } دِ راشي	راتلنه

☞ Note particularly 3rd sing. masc. Imperf. Indic. (2nd form). It is frequently mistaken for راته, "to me," or "to us."

Notes.

راتلل, is irregular in that—

(1) The Pres. Subjunct. is not formed from the Pres. Indic., which itself is irregular.

(2) The Aorist is formed from the Past Participle.

(3) The Past Participle is formed irregularly.

(4) The Potential Mood is formed from what one would naturally suppose would be the Past Participle.

In some parts of the N.-W. Frontier the Potential Mood is actually formed from the Past Participle (Column 4), زه راغلي شم, etc., but this should not be adopted.

To Come.

3

Imperfect Indicative.
(I was coming.)

1st Form.

زه راتللم
ته راتللیَ
(m.) هغه راتلو
(f.) هغه راتله
مونږ راتللو
تاسو راتللئ
هغوئ (m.) راتلل
هغوئ (f.) راتللیَ

2nd Form.

زه راتلم
ته راتلیَ
هغه (m.) راته
هغه (f.) راتله
مونږ راتلو
تاسو راتلئ
هغوئ (m.) راتلل
هغوئ (f.) راتلیَ

Habitual Imperfect.
(I used to come, *or*
I was in the habit of coming.)

1st Form. زه به راتللم

2nd Form. زه به راتلم

etc.

4

Past Participle.
(having come.)

راغلیَ

Perfect Indicative.
(I have come.)

زه راغلیَ یم
etc.
مونږ راغلي یو
etc.

Pluperf. Conditional.
(If I had come.)

که زه راغلیَ ویَ

Doubtful Past.
(I may have come.)

زه راغلیَ به یم
etc.

Pluperf. Indicative.
(I had come.)

زه راغلیَ وم
etc.

Past Subjunctive.
(I would *or* might have come.)

زه راغلیَ به وم
etc.

Aorist.
(I came.)

زه راغلم
هغه (m.) راغیَ
هغه (f.) راغله
هغه (f.) راغه
هغوئ (m.) راغلل
هغوئ (f.) راغللیَ
هغوئ (f.) راغلیَ

5

Present Potential.
(I can come.)

زه راتللیَ *or* راتلیَ شم
etc.

Future Potential.
(I will be able to come.)

زه راتللیَ *or* راتلیَ به شم
etc.

Past Potential.
(I could come.)

زه راتللیَ *or* راتلیَ شوم
etc.

94. Compound of کیدل with a (Verbal) Adjective. روانیدل

1

Pres. Indic. (I set out.)
زه روانیږم
etc.

Weak. (I will set out.)
زه به روانیږم
etc.

Continuous.
ته روانیږه
تاسو روانیږئ

Future.

Imperative.
set thou out.
set ye out.

1a

Pres. Subjunc. (I may set out.)
زه روان شم
etc.

Strong. (I shall set out.)
زه به روان شم
etc.

Definite.
ته روان شه
تاسو روان شئ

Aorist. (I set out.)

1st Form. زه روان شولم

2nd Form. زه روان شوم

etc.

2

Verbal Noun. (the setting out.)
روانیدل

Active Agent.
روانیدونکی he who sets out.
روانیدونکي she who sets out.

Gerund. (a setting out.)
روانیدنه

Notes.

When کیدل is compounded with an Adjective—

(1) the Adjective coalesces with the parent verb in Columns 1, 3 and 5.

(2) it drops the prefixed و of the parent verb in Column 1a.

(3) in those tenses which are formed from the non-existent Infinitive "شول" (i.e. in Columns 1a and 4) the Adjective agrees in Gender and Number with the Noun or Pronoun which is the subject of the Verb.

To Set Out, Start. — **Intransitive Verb.**

3

Imperfect Indicative.
(I was setting out.)

1st Form.	*2nd Form.*
زه روانيدلم	زه روانيدم

etc.

Habitual Imperfect.
(I used to set out, *or* I was in the habit of setting out.)

1st Form.	*2nd Form.*
زه به روانيدلم	زه به روانيدم

etc.

4

Past Participle.
(having set out.)
روان شوي

Perfect Indicative.
(I have set out.)
زه روان شوي يم
etc.

Pluperfect Condit.
(If I had set out.)
كه زه روان شوي وي
etc.

Doubtful Past.
(I may have set out.)
زه روان شوي به يم
etc.

Pluperf. Indicative.
(I had set out.)
زه روان شوي وم
etc.

Past Subjunctive.
(I might *or* would have set out.)
زه روان شوي به وم
etc.

5

Present Potential.
(I can set out.)
زه روانيدلي[1] شم
etc.

Future Potential.
(I shall be able to set out.)
زه روانيدلي[1] به شم
etc.

Past Potential.
(I could set out.)
زه روانيدلي[1] شوم
etc.

---

[1] Or روانيدي

95. Compound of کول with a (Verbal) Adjective. روانول

1

Present Indic.
(I send off.)
زه روانوم
etc.

Future.

Weak.
(I will send off.)
زه به روانوم
etc.

Continuous.
ته روانوه
تاسو روانوئ

Imperative.
send thou off.
send ye off.

1a

Present Subj.
(I may send off.)
زه روان کړم
etc.

Strong.
(I shall send off.)
زه به روان کړم
etc.

Definite.
ته روان کړه
تاسو روان کړئ

Aorist.
(— sent me, you, etc., off.)

روان کړلم
,, کړلې
(*m.*) ,, کړ
(*f.*) روانه کړله
روان کړلو
,, کړلئ
(*m.*) ,, کړل
(*f.*) رواني کړې
,, کړلې

2

Verbal Noun.
(the sending off.)
روانول

Active Agent.
روانونکی he who sends off.
روانونکي she who sends off.

Gerund.
(a sending off.)
روانونه

TO SEND OFF *or* CAUSE TO START. TRANSITIVE VERB.

3

IMPERFECT INDIC.
(— was sending me, you, etc., off.)

روانَولم
روانَولې
روانَوه (*m.*)
روانَوله (*f.*)
روانَولو
روانَولئ
روانَول (*m.*)
روانَولې (*f.*)

HABIT. IMPERF.
(— used to send me, *or* was in the habit of sending me, you, etc., off.)

به روانَولم
etc.

4

PAST PARTICIPLE.
(having sent.)

روان کړي

PERFECT INDICATIVE.
(— has sent me, you, etc., off.)

روان کړيَ يم

PLUPERFECT CONDITIONAL.
(If I had sent off.)

که ما روان کړيَ ويَ

DOUBTFUL PAST.
(— may have sent me off.)

روان کړيَ به يم
etc.

PLUPERFECT INDICATIVE.
(— had sent me.)

روان کړيَ وم
etc.

PAST SUBJUNCTIVE.
(— might have sent me.)

روان کړي به وم
etc.

5

PRES. POTENTIAL.
(I can send off.)

زه روانولَي شم
etc.

FUTURE POTENTIAL.
(I shall be able to send off.)

زه روانولَي به شم
etc.

PAST POTENTIAL.
(— could send me off.)

روانولَي شوم
etc.

NOTES.

When کول is compounded with an Adjective—

(1) the Adjective coalesces with the Verb in Cols. 1, 2, 3, and 5, *and the Adjective takes the short vowel zawar.*

(2) the و of the Parent Verb is dropped in Col. 1A.

(3) ONLY in those tenses which are formed from the non-existent Infinitive "کړل". (i.e. in Cols. 1A and 4) does the Adjective agree in Gender and Number with the Noun or Pronoun which is the Subject of the Verb.

96. گِرزيدل To Wander.

1		1A	2
Present Indic. (I wander.) زهٔ گِرزم etc.		Pres. Subjunc. (I may wander.) زهٔ وُگِرزم etc.	Verbal Noun. (the wandering.) گِرزيدل
Weak. (I will wander.) زهٔ به گِرزم etc.	Future.	Strong. (I shall wander.) زهٔ به وُگِرزم etc.	Active Agent. گِرزيدونکې he who wanders. گِرزيدونکي she who wanders.
Continuous. تهٔ گِرزه تاسو گِرزئ	Imperative. wander thou. wander ye.	Definite. تهٔ وُگِرزه تاسو وُگِرزئ	Gerund. (a wandering.) گِرزيدنه

INTRANSITIVE VERB.

3

IMPERFECT INDICATIVE.
(I was wandering.)
زه گِرزيدام
etc.

HABITUAL IMPERFECT.
(I used to wander *or* I was in the habit of wandering.)
زه به گِرزيدم
etc.

AORIST.
(I wandered.)
زه وُگِرزيدم
etc.

4

PAST PARTICIPLE.
(having wandered.)
گِرزيدلَي

PERFECT INDICATIVE.
(I have wandered.)
زه گِرزيدلَي يم
etc.

PLUPERFECT CONDITIONAL.
(If I had wandered.)
كه زه گِرزيدلَي وَي

DOUBTFUL PAST.
(I may have wandered.)
زه گِرزيدلَي به يم
etc.

PLUPERFECT INDICATIVE.
(I had wandered.)
زه گِرزيدلَي وم
etc.

PAST SUBJUNCTIVE.
(I might *or* would have wandered.)
زه گِرزيدلَي به وم
etc.

PRESENT POTENTIAL.
(I can wander.)
زه گِرزيدلَي شم
etc.

FUTURE POTENTIAL.
(I shall be able to wander.)
زه گِرزيدلَي به شم
etc.

PAST POTENTIAL.
(I could wander.)
زه گِرزيدلَي شوم
etc.

97. لویدل TO FALL.

1		1A	2
PRES. INDICATIVE. (I fall.) زه لویږم etc.		PRES. SUBJUNCTIVE. (I may fall.) زه ولویږم etc.	VERBAL NOUN. (the falling.) لویدل
WEAK. (I will fall.) زه به لویږم etc.	FUTURE.	STRONG. (I shall fall.) زه به ولویږم etc.	ACTIVE AGENT. لویدونکی he who falls.
CONTINUOUS. ته لویږه تاسو لویږئ	IMPERATIVE. fall thou. fall ye.	DEFINITE. ته ولویږه تاسو ولویږئ	GERUND. (a falling.) لویدنه

98. استول TO SEND.

1		1A	2
PRES. INDICATIVE. (I send.) زه استوم etc.		PRES. SUBJUNCTIVE. (I may send.) زه واستوم etc.	VERBAL NOUN. (the sending.) استول
WEAK. (I will send.) زه به استوم etc.	FUTURE.	STRONG. (I shall send.) زه به واستوم etc.	ACTIVE AGENT. استونکی he who sends.
CONTINUOUS. ته استوه تاسو استوئ	IMPERATIVE. send thou. send ye.	DEFINITE. ته واستوه تاسو واستوئ	GERUND. (a sending.) استونه

INTRANSITIVE VERB.

3

IMPERFECT INDICATIVE.
(I was falling.)
زه لویدم
etc.

HABITUAL IMPERFECT.
(I used to fall, *or* I was in the habit of falling.)
زه به لویدم
etc.

AORIST.
(I fell.)
زه ولویدم
etc.

4

PAST PARTICIPLE.
(having fallen.)
لویدلي

PERFECT INDICATIVE.
(I have fallen.)
زه لویدلي یم
etc.

PLUPERFECT CONDITIONAL.
(If I had fallen.)
که زه لویدلي وَيَ

and so on for all other tenses.

TRANSITIVE VERB.

3

IMPERFECT INDICATIVE.
(— was sending me, you, etc.)
استَولم
استَوه (*m.*)
استَوله (*f.*)
استَول (*m.*)
استَولیَ (*f.*)

HABITUAL IMPERFECT.
(— used to send, *or* was in the habit of sending, me, you, etc.)
به استَولم
etc.

AORIST.
(— sent me, you, etc.)
واستَولم
etc.

4

PAST PARTICIPLE.
(having sent.)
استَولي

PERFECT INDICATIVE.
(— has sent me.)
استَولیَ یم

PLUPERFECT CONDITIONAL.
(If I had sent.)
که ما استَولیَ ويَ

and so on for all other tenses.

99. بيول / بوتلل } To Lead or Take Away (of Animate Objects).

1 — 1A — 2

Pres. Indicative.
زه بيايم

Weak.
زه به بيايم

Continuous.
ته بيايه

Future.

Imperative.

Pres. Subjunctive.
زه بوزم

Strong.
زه به بوزم

Definite.
ته بوزه

Verbal Noun.
بيول
(بوتلل)

Active Agent.
بيونكي
(بوتلونكي)

Gerund.
بيونه
(بوتلنه)

100. وړل To Carry or Take Away (of Inanimate Objects).

1 — 1A — 2

Pres. Indicative.
زه وړم

Weak.
زه به وړم

Continuous.
ته وړه

Future.

Imperative.

Pres. Subjunctive.
زه يوسم

Strong.
زه به يوسم

Definite
ته يوسه

Aorist.
يوړم
يوَړ 3rd Sing.

Verbal Noun.
وړل

Active Agent.
وړونكي

Gerund.
وړنه

Defective Transitive Verb.

3

Imperfect Indicative.

بیوم
(بوتلم)

Habitual Imperfect.

دہ بیوم
(دہ بوتلم)

Aorist.

بوتلم

☛ بوت 3rd Sing.

4

Past Participle.

بیولیَ
(بوتلیَ)

Perfect Indicative.

بیولیَ یم

↓

and so on for all other tenses.

☛ The forms in brackets, though occasionally met with, should not be adopted.

Defective Transitive Verb.

3

Imperfect Indicative.

وڈم

Habitual Imperfect.

دہ وڈم

4

Past Participle.

وڈیَ

Perfect Indicative.

وڈیَ یم

↓

and so on for all other tenses.

101. راوړل To Bring

1		1A	2
Pres. Indicative. راوړم		Pres. Subjunctive. راوړم	Verbal Noun. راوړل
Weak. به راوړم	Future.	Strong. بهٔ راوړم	Active Agent. راوړونکي
Continuous. راوړه	Imperat.	Definite. راوړه	Gerund. راوړنه

102. نیول To Catch.

1		1A	2
Pres. Indicative. نیسم or نسم		Pres. Subjunctive. ونیسم	Verbal Noun. نیول
Weak. به نیسم	Future.	Strong. به ونیسم	Active Agent. نیونکي
Continuous. ته نیسه	Imperat.	Definite. ته ونیسه	Gerund. نیونه

103. کیښودل To Place *or* Put.

1		1A	2
Pres. Indicative. ږدم		Pres. Subjunctive. کیږدم	Verbal Noun. کیښودل
Weak. به ږدم	Future.	Strong. به کیږدم	Active Agent. کیښودونکي
Continuous. ته ږده	Imperat.	Definite. ته کیږده[1]	Gerund. کیښودنه

[1] Colloquially کیده.

(of Inanimate Objects).

3

- Imperfect Indicative.
  - راوڕم
- Habitual Imperfect.
  - به راوڕم
- Aorist.
  - راوڕم
  - راوڕ (3rd Sing.)

4

- Past Participle.
  - راوڕيَ
- Perfect Indicative.
  - راوڕي يم
- ↓ and so on for all other tenses.

Transitive Verb.

3

- Imperfect Indicative.
  - نيوم
- Habitual Imperfect.
  - به نيوم
- Aorist.
  - ونيوم

4

- Past Participle.
  - نيوليَ
- Perfect Indicative.
  - نيوليَ يم
- ↓ and so on for all the other tenses.

Transitive Verb.

3

- Imperfect Indicative.
  - كينبودم
- Habitual Imperfect.
  - به كينبودم
- Aorist.
  - Same as Imperf. Indic.

4

- Past Participle.
  - ☞ ايبنيَ
  - or
  - كينبودليَ
- Perfect Indic.
  - ايبني يم
  - or
  - كينبودلي يم
- ↓ and so on for all other tenses of this Column, *excluding the Potential Mood.*

5

- Pres. Potential.
  - ☞ ايبنويَ شم
  - or
  - كينبودليَ شم
- ↓ and similarly for the other tenses of the Potential Mood.

104. ويستل or يستل } To Extract.

1		1A	2
Pres. Indicative. وباسم		Pres. Subjunctive. وُباسم	Verbal Noun. ويستل
Weak. به وباسم	Future.	Strong. به وُباسم	Active Agent. ويستونکي
Continuous. ته وباسه	Imperat.	Definite. ته وُباسه	Gerund. ويستنه

105. راخکل راکښل راښکل } To Pull.

1		1A	2
Pres. Indicative. راکاږم		Pres. Subjunctive. راکاږم	Verbal Noun. راخکل
Weak. به راکاږم	Future.	Strong. به راکاږم	Active Agent. راخکونکي
Continuous. ته راکاږه	Imperat.	Definite. ته راکاږه	Gerund. راخکنه

TRANSITIVE VERB.

3

IMPERFECT INDICATIVE.
ويستم
↓
HABITUAL IMPERFECT.
ده ويستم
↓
AORIST.
وويستم

4

PAST PARTICIPLE.
ويستلي or ويستي
↓
and so on for all other tenses.

TRANSITIVE VERB.

3

IMPERFECT INDICATIVE.
راخكم
↓
HABITUAL IMPERFECT.
به راخكم
↓
AORIST.
Same as Imperf. Indic.

4

PAST PARTICIPLE.
راخكي
↓
and so on for all other tenses.

106. ويل To Say *or* Speak.

- **1**
  - Pres. Indicative. وايم or ويم
    - Future. Weak. به وايم or به ويم
      - Imperative. Continuous. ته وايه / تاسو وايئ
  - **1A**
    - Pres. Subjunctive. ؤوايم
      - Future. Strong. به ؤوايم
        - Imperative. Definite. ته ؤوايه / تاسو ؤوايئ
- **2**
  - Verbal Noun. ويل
    - Active Agent. ويونكىَ
      - Gerund. وينه

Notes.

(1) In Past tenses this verb can only be used in the 3rd persons Singular and Plural.

(2) In Past tenses where ؤو occurs, in either Number or in either Gender, it is preferable to denote the Agent by the short forms (para. 116) when it is a personal pronoun; in which case the ؤو is separated, and the Agent is placed between; e.g.—

ؤ مِ وِ or ؤ مِ ويل I said; ؤ ئي وِ or ؤ ئي ويل he said.

سندرىَ ؤ ئي ويلې they sang songs.

Transitive Verb.

3

Imperfect Indicative.

- Sing.: (m.) وُوِ or وِ; (f.) وُويله
- Plur.: (m.) وُويل or ويل; (f.) وُويلي

Habitual Imperfect.

- Sing.: (m.) به وُوِ or به وِ; (f.) به وُويله
- Plur.: (m.) به وُويل or به ويل; (f.) به وُويلَي

Aorist.

Same as Imperf. Indicative.

4

Past Participle.

ويلَي

Perfect Indicative.

- Sing.: ويلَي (m.) دَي; (f.) دَه
- Plur.: ويلِي دِي

Pluperfect Conditional.

كه ما ويلَي وَي

Doubtful Past.

- Sing.: ويلَي (m.) به وِي; (f.) به وَه
- Plur.: ويلِي به وِي

Pluperfect Indicative.

- Sing.: ويلَي (m.) وُه; (f.) وَه
- Plur.: ويلِي (m.) وُو; (f.) وَي

Past Subjunctive.

- Sing.: ويلَي به (m.) وُه; (f.) وَه
- Plur.: ويلِي به (m.) وُو; (f.) وَي

Present Potential.

زه ويلَي شم

Future Potential.

زه ويلَي به شم

Past Potential.

- Sing.: ويلَي (m.) شه; (f.) شوله / شوه
- Plur.: ويلِي (m.) شول; (f.) شولَي / شوي

107. In addition to the irregular verbs given in paras. 84, 86 and 108, and those conjugated in the preceding pages, the following verbs form some of their tenses irregularly :—

Remarks.	Past Participle.	Aorist.	Imperfect Indicative.	Present Indicative.	Infinitive.
				آغږم	اخل to knead.
				اوم	اودل to weave.
				بُلم or بولم	بلل to call.
			پرېښودلم پرېښودم	پرېږدم	پرېښودل to let go.
				پُښتم	پُښتیدل to be asked.
This verb is practically obsolete.				پیرم	پیرودل to buy.
				پیژنم	پیژندل to recognise.
چوم is also the Pres. Indic. of the Trans. verb چول, *to split.*				چوم	چاودل to split (*intransitive*).
				خرایم	خریل to shave.
ړ is replaced by ر in Columns 1 and 1A.				خورم	خوړل to eat.
				خوځم	خوځیدل to move.
This verb borrows its Pres. Indic. from ریبل, *to reap.*				ریبم	رودل to reap.
				روم	رودل to suck.

Very rarely used.	زغلیدلی[1] or زغاښتی زغاښدتلی[2]	و زغلیدم[1] و زغاښتم[2]	زعیدم[1] زغاښتم[2]	زغلم	زغلیدل	to run.
				زیږم	زیږیدل	to be born.
				سپړم	سپړودل	to unravel.
				سکښم	سکښتل	to shear or cut out (clothes).
				سکنړم	سکنړودل	to clip.
	سوزولی سوئی	سوزولم		سوزوم	سوزول سول	to burn (*transitive*).
				سوزم	سوزیدل	to burn (*intransitive*).
	ښولی or ښیلی		ښوولم or ښولم	ښایم or ښیم	ښایل ښیل ښوول	to show.
				غړم	غښتل	to coil.
				گورم	کتل	to look.
				وینم	لیدل	to see.
				مومم	مُندل or موندل	to find.
				وژنم or وجنم	وژل or وجل	to kill.

[1] Ordinary forms.

[2] Afridi and Khattack forms.

108. The following Verbs form a class by themselves as regards the way in which they form their Present Indicative :—

PRESENT INDICATIVE.	INFINITIVE.	
جاړم	جړل (ژړل)	to weep.
خاندم	خندل	to laugh.
ڈانگم	دنگل	to leap.
غاپم	غپل	to bark.
لانبم	لنبل	to bathe.
ناړم	نړل	to shout.
نغاړم	نغړودل	to swallow.

109. Many dissyllabic Infinitives insert a long vowel (ا) in the 3rd Singular Aorist; as :—

AORIST (3RD SINGULAR).	INFINITIVE.	
وتاړه	تړل	to bind.
وچاوه	چول	to split.
وکاته	کتل	to look.
وکاره	کرل	to sow.

etc., etc.

But this is not confined to dissyllabic Infinitives. E.g. :—

واچاوه	اچول	to place.
واستاوه	استول	to send.
ولګاوه	لګول	to reach, hit.
ونښلاوه	نښلول	to raise.

etc.

The above forms are *in addition to* the regularly derived short forms,—وتړه , وچوه , وکته , وکره , واچوه , واستوه etc., etc.

ON THE CONSTRUCTION OF A SENTENCE CONTAINING A PAST TENSE OF A TRANSITIVE VERB.

110. It has been stated in para. 81 that the suffixes of tenses of Intransitive Verbs, and of Present and Future tenses of Transitive Verbs, denote the Subjec of the sentence. But when we come to Past tenses of Transitive Verbs the same rule does not hold good.

In these cases the terminations of the Verb (which, by the way, are exactly the same as those mentioned in para. 81) denote what in English would be called the Object, while the Subject of the English sentence becomes in Pushtu the Agent, and is consequently put into the Instrumental case (para. 15 (8)), and *the Verb agrees in Gender, Number and Person with the Object.*

The following examples will explain the construction :—

By the man I (was) hit.	سړيِ زه وُوهلم	The man hit me.
„ thou (wast) hit.	سړيِ ته وُوهلې	The man hit thee.
„ the horse (was) hit.	سړيِ آس وُوهه	The man hit the horse.
„ the woman (was) hit.	سړيِ ښځه وُوهله	The man hit the woman.
„ we (were) hit.	سړيِ مونږ وُوهلو	The man hit us.
„ you (were) hit.	سړيِ تاسو وُوهلئ	The man hit you.
„ the horses (were) hit.	سړيِ آسونه وُوهل	The man hit the horses.
„ the women (were) hit.	سړي ښځې وُوهلې	The man hit the women.

111. In the right-hand column "the man" in each English sentence is the Subject of the verb "hit"; while "me," "thee," "the horse," etc., are respectively the Objects of the various sentences.

When, however, these sentences are rendered into Pushtu the Subject of the English sentence is put into the Instrumental case—سړيِ *by the man,*—and the verb agrees in Gender, Number and Person with the Object of the English sentence.

Hence we see that in Past Tenses of Transitive Verbs the suffixes indicate the object "on which the action falls."

112. By covering the words سړيِ in the middle column of para. 111 it will appear as if we had a regularly conjugated tense of a regular Intransitive verb. *And so we have,* but with two fundamental differences between Intransitive and Past tenses of Transitive Verbs.

113. At the risk of repetition (which must be pardoned, seeing how important the point is), these differences will be shown side by side.

Past Tenses of Transitive Verbs.		Other tenses of Transitive and all tenses of Intransitive Verbs.
The Verb contains an incomplete sentence : زهٔ وُوهلم . . . . struck me.	(1)	The Verb contains a complete sentence : زهٔ ځم I go.
The suffix indicates the *Object* of the Verb.	(2)	The suffix indicates the *Subject* of the Verb.

Therefore, since Past tenses of Transitive Verbs are incomplete without an Instrumental case to denote the Agent, it will be understood why incomplete meanings have been given to such tenses in the Verbs conjugated out on the preceding pages, and which have been printed in special type, that attention may be drawn to them.

114. The simplest way of explaining the construction of the Pushtu sentences in para. 110 would be to say that the English sentence must be turned from the Active Voice (right-hand column) to the Passive (left-hand column). But this is not correct, for the Verb in Pushtu is Active, not Passive. It is, however, a convenient way of arriving at the Agent and the Object.

Perhaps a better explanation would be as follows (taking the first and last sentences of the examples in para. 110 as illustrations) :—

The man hit me. "The man," Instrumental case.
"hit," Aorist tense.
"me," 1st person Singular.

∴ the Verb must be put into the 1st person Singular, Aorist tense.

The man hit the women. "The man hit," as above.
"the women," 3rd person Feminine Plural.

∴ the Verb must be put into the 3rd person Feminine Plural, Aorist tense.

115. We have seen from paras. 110 and 111 that in Past tenses of Transitive Verbs the Subject of the sentence is not inherent in the Pushtu Verb. It is therefore *absolutely necessary that the Agent in such cases should be expressed.*

Example :—
"The King collected an army, killed his son, and reigned in his stead."

We will cut this up into its component parts, and examine each in detail, to enable us to arrive at the Pushtu equivalents.

(1) *The King collected an army.*

"Collected," Aorist tense of a Transitive Verb, therefore we must adopt the construction given in para. 110. The sentence will now become, "By the King an army (was) collected." "Army," 3rd pers. sing. masc.; therefore the Verb "collected" will be in the 3rd pers. sing. masc. Aorist, and we get :—

بادشاهٔ لښکر جمع کړ

(2) *Killed his son.*

"Killed," Aorist tense of a Transitive Verb, with Nominative (Subject) "the King" understood in English from the previous sentence. But, as we have seen, in Pushtu the Subject becomes the Agent, and the Agent *must* be expressed. In this case it will be by the Personal Pronoun ئي, "*by him.*" The rest of the sentence will be constructed as in (1), and we get in Pushtu :—

خپل ځوئي وئي وژه

(3) *And reigned in his stead.*

"Reigned," an Intransitive Verb. The terminal letter of a tense in a finite mood of an Intransitive Verb itself designates the Subject (or Nominative) of the Verb, so that nothing further is needed, and the sentence is translated in a straightforward manner, thus :—

او په ځائي کښې ئي کښيناست

116. The Instrumental cases of the Personal Pronouns, which have to be used in connection with Past tenses of Transitive Verbs, have already been given in the various paragraphs dealing with Personal Pronouns; but it will be convenient to collect and tabulate them here.

		SINGULAR.	PLURAL.
1st Person		م , ما	مو , موږ
2nd ,,		دِ , تا	مو , تاسو or تاسي
3rd ,,	(masc.) هغهٔ / (fem.) هغې	ئي	ئي , هغوئي or هغو

The Instrumental and Possessive cases must not be confounded. It is not always easy to distinguish them, as the short forms are the same in both cases.

117. When the short forms of the Instrumental cases of Personal Pronouns are used, the verb should be divided, and the Instrumental case placed between the divided parts of the verb.

Examples :—

وُ مِ وَيِ	I said.
زه وُ ئي وهلم	He struck me.
وُ مو وهل	We struck them.

118. The Object of a Transitive Verb is frequently omitted in English. *In Pushtu it must be expressed.*

Can you give us any bread to eat ?

مونږ له ډوډئي راكولي شي چه ئي وخورو

(Can you give us bread, that we may eat IT ?)

119. The following Verbs have a peculiar construction in Past tenses :—

توكل	to spit.	زنګل	to swing.
ټوخل	to cough.	غپل	to bark.
ژړل (ژړل)	to weep.	كتل	to look at, gaze.
خندل	to laugh.	كنځل كول	to abuse.
ډنګل	to jump.	لنبل	to bathe.

With these Verbs the Subject of the English sentence becomes in Pushtu the Agent, and the verb itself is used in the 3rd person masculine Plural of the appropriate tense.

Examples :—

هغه په ډرئي و توكل	He spat on the carpet.
ټوله شپه ئي ټوخل	He kept on coughing all night long.
مونږ وژړل	We wept.
ما ورپوري وخندل	I laughed at them.
آس م په ښه شان وډنګل	My horse jumped well.
ماشومانو په باغ كښ زنګل	The children were swinging in the garden.
سپي وغپل	The dog barked.
تا ولي راته وكتل[1]	Why did you stare at me ?

[1] وكته would also be correct.

هغې به خښتن ته کنځل کول She was in the habit of abusing her husband.

هلک په سیند کښ لنبل The boy was bathing in the river.

120. On the use of شته and دي.

شته = is *or* are. 3rd Singular and Plural. Masculine and Feminine. It is used instead of دي when Interrogation or Affirmation is required to be expressed, *with reference to objects remote or absent, or if there is a doubt about the existence of an object.*

تا ځخه توپک شته که نه Have you a gun?

شته Yes, I have.

دي = is. 3rd Singular. Masculine. Definite Present. It is used with reference to objects *actually present*—that is to say, where there is no doubt as to the existence of the thing mentioned but there is a doubt as to whose it is.

دا دَ چا توپک دي Whose gun is this?

شته دي, conjoined, are used when special emphasis is desired to be expressed.

کلي ته لار شته که نه Is there a road to the village?

شته دي Yes, certainly (of course) there is.

The Negative form of شته is نشته.

121. The Difference between دي and وي.

دي (or دي) is the Definite Present.

کليوال ډير ناوزګار دي The villagers are very busy.

This implies that the villagers are very busy NOW, but that they will not be so in a day or two.

وي is the Habitual or Continuous Present.

په اوړي او مني کښ کليوال ډير ناوزګار وي The villagers are very busy during the summer and autumn.

The force of وي here is that *every summer and autumn* the villagers are very busy.

وي is also the 3rd Singular or Plural of the Future tense of the Auxiliary Verb. Where used thus it sometimes implies doubt or probability.

هغه به کور وي که نه Will he be in? Is he at home?

هغه به وي He may be in, *or* He probably is in.

وي is also used in Conditional sentences.

که هلته وي نو زه به ور سره خبرې وکړم If he is there I will speak to him.

Prohibition and Negation.

122. *Prohibition* is expressed by the particle مه with the Continuous Imperative (for the 2nd Person, i.e. for the True Imperative).

The particle is usually written as a separate word.

مه کوئي Do not do.

But sometimes it is found joined to the verb by the elision of the ه.

مکوئي

This latter form should not be copied.

123. In the ordinary every-day greetings used by Pathans we have the particle مه joined with the Subjunctive Mood, and even to the Indicative. In these cases we must regard the مه not as a prohibition, but the whole phrase as being in the Optative Mood.

ستړې مه شې May you not be weary!

مه خوارېږې / خوار مه شې } May you not become poor!

124. With the 1st and 3rd Persons the Negative particle نه is used.

له کور نه هغه دِ بهر نه وزي Do not let him leave the house.

125. *Negation* is expressed by the particle نه.

1. In Present and Future tenses it precedes the verb.

نه لولم I do not read.

2. In tenses which prefix و the negative particle is placed between the و and the rest of the verb.

و نه لولم I may not read.

3. In Past tenses the verb *must be divided,* and the Negative particle interposed between the two parts, the particle frequently coälescing with the verb by dropping the ه.

هغه را نغيَ (= هغه نه راغيَ)	He did not come.
هغه وا نه ستوه (= نه واستوه)	He did not send it.
و نه ليکه (= نه وليکه)	He did not write.
هغه پرېَ نه وت	He did not fall.
هغه پورېَ نه وت	He did not cross.
هغه څم نه لاست	He did not lie down.
هغه کښېَ نه ناست	He did not sit.

4. In compound tenses the negative particle precedes the auxiliary verb.

هغه زه نه يم ساتلېَ هغه زه ساتلېَ نه يم	He did not protect me.

Continued Action.

126. Continued action is expressed by repetition, introduced by the particle په.

په ډو ډو راغيَ	He came running.
دَ سيند په غاړه غاړه لاړ شه	He went along the river bank.
په شپه شپه	During the night.

But—

په پټو پټو کښې لاړم	I went along the fields.

The کښې is introduced here because the sense is "through the fields." In the second example, above, "the river bank" is a well-defined line, but "the fields" is not a defined line.

The following examples may make the difference clearer :—

دا سړيَ زما په پټو پټو کښې لاړ او فصلونه م خراب ئي کړل	This man went through my fields, and spoilt my crops.
نه - ستا په پټو پټو کښې لا نه ړم ليکن په پولو پولو	No; I did not go through your fields, but (went) along the boundaries.

127. In a narrative, *when no particular time is mentioned,* the Verb in Pushtu must be in a Past tense *other than the Pluperfect,* although the Pluperfect has been used in English.

يو څو سړي دلته راغلل او چه لاړل راته معلومه شوه چه يو آس مِ ئي غلا کړ	Some men came here, and after they *had* gone I found that they *had* stolen one of my horses.

But when a particular period of time is mentioned in conjunction with *any* past tense in English, the Verb in Pushtu *must be in the Pluperfect tense.*

پرون يوڅو سړي راغلي وُو او چه لاړل ماښام راته معلومه شوه چه يو آس مِ ئي غلا کړي وُه	Some men came yesterday, and after they had gone I found out in the evening that they had stolen one of my horses.

Two Verbs joined by the Conjunction "And."

128. When two Verbs are joined by the conjunction "and" the Pushtu idiom is exactly like the English.

It does not follow the Urdu rule of putting the first verb into the Past Participle, dropping the conjunction, and putting the second verb into a finite tense.

هغه دلته راغيَ او را سره ئي خبريَ وکړيَ	He came here and spoke to me.

Oratio Obliqua and Oratio Recta.

129. In English, when repeating a conversation or the words used by a person, we can employ either the Oratio Obliqua or the Oratio Recta, as we please. In Pushtu, however, the Oratio Recta alone can be used; that is, the actual words spoken by the person quoted must be given, introduced by the particle چه, "*that.*"

وايي چه زه به ځم	He says that he will go.
ته وائي چه ما هغه و نه ليده	You say that you did not see him.
له هغه سړي نه تپوس وکړه چه نوم دِ څه دي	Ask that man his name.

Let us imagine a man charged with assaulting a woman, and the woman giving evidence. The magistrate, in repeating to the accused the woman's statement, would say, according to English ideas: "She says that you struck her." In Pushtu he would have to turn the sentence so as to use the very words of the woman:—

ښځه وايي چه وئي وهلم	The woman says that "*he struck me.*"

On the Use of تلل, *to go*, and راتلل, *to come*.

130. These two Verbs must be used in Pushtu with greater care than we use them in English.

Let us suppose that two men, A and B, are talking together, and that A, who lives at "a," says to B: "Last night I went to C's house." This would have to be rendered into Pushtu, "Last night I *came* to C's house;" because C's house is nearer to the speakers.

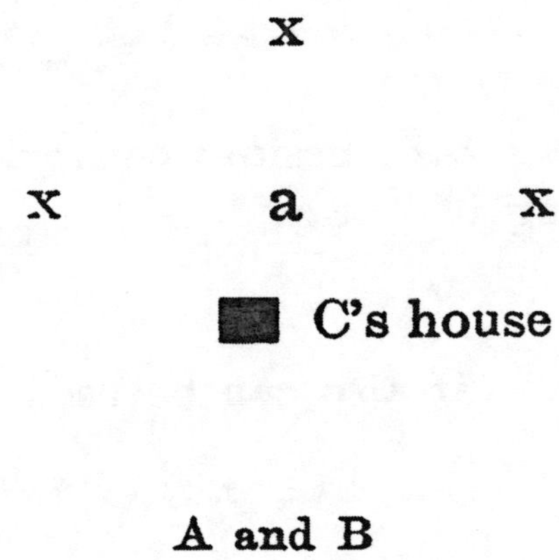

If the place visited had been in another position, such as x, A would have used the words "I went."

Possession—how expressed.

131. "Possession" is expressed in various ways.

1. The verb لرل, "*to have*," is complete in its Present and Future tenses. The Past tenses, which are formed regularly, can be used only in the 3rd persons Singular and Plural.

Aorist.		Imperfect.	
ولرۀ	(masc.)	لرۀ	Singular.
ولرله	(fem.)	لرله	
ولرل	(masc.)	لرل	Plural.
ولرلي	(fem.)	لرلي	

2. شته is used exactly like the Urdu کے پاس, and requires the inflected case when used with a Noun or Personal Pronoun; e.g.:

ما شته	I have.	هغه شته	he has.
تا شته	you have.	هغې شته	she has.

etc.

3. The above construction, however, cannot be used with reference to a human being. In such cases the idiom is as follows:—

ځوئي دِ شته که نه Have you a son? (*Does your son exist?*)

4. When an abstract quality is referred to, the idiom is again different :—

پہ دي کښ ځما شک دي I am doubtful about this. (*In this my doubt is.*)

دا آس ځما خوښ دي I like this horse. (*My liking is for this horse.*)

دغه ډوډۍ ځما خوښه نه ده I have no liking for this food.

څخه, besides conveying the meaning of possession, frequently has the meaning of "*near*."

کلي څخه *near* the village.

It also can be used in another sense :—

چا څخه سبق ؤوايو *To whom* should we say our lessons?

CHAPTER III.

ADVERBS

(*including Adverbial Phrases*).

132. *Of Time.*

اخر ,عاقبت ,خو	at last.
اوس	now.
برايه[1]	last night.
بل صبا	day after to-morrow.
بله شپه	next night.
بيا	again.
بيګاه	last night.
بيګاله	to-night.
پخوا ,ورږنبي	formerly.
پرون	yesterday.
پس ,پسته ,پسي[2]	after, next.
په دي شپو ورځو کښي	nowadays.
تر اوس پوري	until now.
تر دي وقت پوري	hitherto.
تر . . . . . پوري	until.
تر څو پوري ,کمه پوري	how long?
تل ,تل تر تله	for ever.
تل ,مدام ,هرکله	always.
چري	ever, at any time.

چه	when, while.
دَ شپي	by night.
دَ مياشتِ	monthly.
دَ ورځي	by day.
ډير ځلَ	often.
صباله	to-morrow.
کله	when ?
کله چه	whenever.
کله راسي	since when.
کله کله	sometimes, seldom.
کله نه کله	now and then.
لا ورمِه ورځ	three days ago.
ناوقت ,ناوخت	late.
نن	to-day.
وقتي ,وختي	early.
ورمه ورځ	day before yesterday.
ورږنبي ,ورږاندِ[2]	before.
هاله	then.
هدو چري نه ,هيڅ چري	never.
هرکال	yearly.
هره مياشت	every month.
هره ورځ	daily.

[1] Used by Kākars.

[2] Takes له . . . . نه

133. *Of Place.*

باندِ	on, upon.
بل ځاي	somewhere.
بل چرته	elsewhere.
بهر	outside.
بیرته	back, backwards.
په .... کښ	in.
په مینځ کښ	among, in the midst of.
پورته, دَ پاسَ	above, on, over.
تر[1]	to, as far as.
تر .... پوري	up to.
تر دي ځاي پوري	to this place, hither.
تر هغه ځاي پوري	to that place, thither.
چرته	where.
دلته هلته	here and there.
دلي, دلته	here.
دننه	inside.
دي خوا	this way.
گیرچاپیر[2]	round about.
لاندِ, دَ لاندِ	below, under.
لاندِ باندِ	upside down.
لري	far.
له دي ځاي نه	from this place, hence.
له کم ځاي نه	from which place, whence.
له ورایه	from afar (*as regards sight*).
له هغه ځاي نه	from that place, thence.
نږدي	near.
ورستو[2]	behind.
وړاندِ[2]	in front.
هرچرته	everywhere.
هغه خوا	that way.
هوري, هلته	there.
هیچرته	nowhere.

134. *Of Manner.*

بي له .... نه, بي	without.
په باندِ	against.
په پټه, په غلا	secretly.
په تلوار, زر زر	quickly.
په جار, په څرگنده, په ظاهره	openly.
په حق, په حلاله, په روا	rightly, justly.
په ناروا, په ناحقه, په دروغه	wrongly, unjustly, falsely.
په خراب شان	badly.
په ښه شان, په ښه رنگ	carefully, well.
په قلار	quietly.
په قلار, رورو, په رورو	slowly.
په قستن, قصداً	purposely.
په گډوډ حال	higgledy-piggledy.
په گرانه سره, په ربړ سره	with difficulty.
تار پتار, دانه وانه	helter-skelter.
څنگه, څه رنگ	how.
خو	at least.

---

[1] When تر is used with a Noun ending in a consonant, the Noun inflects by the addition of the short vowel *zawar*, ترکابلَ, "as far as Kabul."

[2] Takes له .... نه

خواه مخواه willy-nilly.
سره together.
که نه وي otherwise.
لکه for instance.
ناڅاپه, ناګهانه suddenly.
يواځي alone.

135. *Of Degree.*

بلکه moreover.
بي حدَ unlimited.
بي شانَ ډير very much indeed.
بيدو exactly.
په قدر قدر little by little.
تر دي پوري to this extent.
تر هسي حدَ پوري to the utmost.
تر هغه پوري to that extent.
څو, څومره how much.
خالي, صِرف only.
دومره, هومره this much.
ډير very.
ډير, بس enough.
ډير ځل very often.
زيات more.
لا even, yet.
لا زيات even more.
لکوتي a little.
هر every.
هرڅو however many.
هرڅه whatever.
هريو everyone.

136. *Of Cause.*

بي هيڅ for no reason.
په دي چه, ځکه, چه, ځکه for this reason, because.

څه دَ پاره for what reason.
څه له, وَلي why?
جوړ, خود accordingly, of course
سره دَ دي notwithstanding, in spite of.
ګُندِ, ګنړه perhaps.
له دي کبلَ, د دي سببَ therefore.

137. *Of Order.*

بيا again.
بي له ..... نه except.
پس after, next.
دوه ځلَ twice.
دويم secondly.
وار په وار in turn.
ورستي, اخر last.
وړنبي firstly.
يوځلَ once.
يو يو one by one.

138. *Of Affirmation.*

بي شکَ, خو certainly, without doubt.
رښتيا in truth.
هو yes.

139. *Of Negation.*

مه do not.
نه no, not.
هډو نه, له سره, بالکل, بيخي not at all.

140. CONJUNCTIONS.

او and	که نه وي ,او که otherwise.
بلکه moreover.	نه وي نو
ځکه ,پس therefore.	لیکن ,ولې but.
ځکه چه because.	نو then.
چه that, for.	هُم also, ever.
چه when.	ولې then.
سره له دې notwithstanding.	یا either, or.
که if.	

PREPOSITIONS.

141. Prepositions are prefixes and suffixes which precede or follow or enclose nouns in order to limit their meanings; e.g.:—

پهٔ سترګو with the eyes.
سړي سره along with the man.
پهٔ کور کښې in the house.

142. The Prepositions in general use are :—

څخه with, at, near.	پرِ on.
د of.	پهٔ on, upon, at.
دَ پاره for, on account of.	پهٔ . . . . کښې in.
سره along with.	ترِ from.
له, له . . . . نه from.	تهٔ to.

143. INTERJECTIONS OR EXCLAMATIONS.

الله O God!	توبه For shame! God forbid! Pardon!
امان Mercy!	خیر Well!
امین May it be so!	شاباش Bravo!
ائې Oh!	وائې وائې Alas, alas!
بارې Very well then!	
بیدار شه Look out!	ورک شه ,دُځه ورک شه Be off!

THE CALENDAR.

144. The Pushtu names for the lunar months of the ordinary Mohammedan Calendar are :—

دَ حسن حسين مياشت	consisting of	30	days.
دَ صفرِي مياشت	,,	29	,,
وړنبي خور	,,	30	,,
دويمه خور	,,	30	,,
دريمه خور	,,	30	,,
څلورمه خور	,,	29	,,
زبرگه (or دَ خدائي) مياشت	,,	30	,,
شوقدر	,,	29	,,
دَ روجي مياشت	,,	30	,,
دَ وروكي اختر مياشت	,,	29	,,
ميانه	,,	30	,,
د لوئي اختر مياشت	,,	29	,,
	Total	355	days.

145. For agricultural purposes, a year of 355 days is most inconvenient. The Hindu Calendar is, therefore, universally employed.

هاړ	corresponding to	June.	پوه	corresponding to	December.
پشكال	,,	July.	ماه	,,	January.
بادرو	,,	August.	پگڼر	,,	February.
اسو	,,	September.	چيتر	,,	March.
كتك	,,	October.	ويساك	,,	April.
مگر	,,	November.	جيټ	,,	May.

146. The Seasons are :—

پسرلي or سپرلي		Spring.		*February, March, April.*
اوړي	اوړي	Hot weather	Summer.	*May, June.*
	پشكال	Rains.		*July, August.*
مني		Autumn.		*September, October.*
ژمي		Winter.		*Nov., Dec., January.*

147. The Days of the Week are :—

دَ خالي ورځ	Saturday.
دَ اتوار (or اتبار) ورځ	Sunday.
دَ ګل (or پير) ورځ	Monday.
دَ نهي ورځ	Tuesday.
چارشنبه (or دَ شروع) ورځ	Wednesday.
دَ زيارت ورځ	Thursday.
جمعه	Friday.

148. Subdivisions of the Day and Night :—

مُلا بانګ مال	the mullah's early call to prayer, one hour before sunrise.
چرګ بانګ مال	cockcrow; half an hour later than the above.
سحر	from dawn till the sun is fully risen.
څاخت	8 to 10 a.m.
غرمه	10 a.m. to 12 noon.
تکنړه غرمه	noon.
ما ُخپښين	afternoon prayer. 2 to 3 p.m.
مازيګر	prayer before sunset. 5 p.m.
ماښام	prayer after sunset. 8 p.m.
ما ُخښتن	night prayer. 10 p.m.
نيمه شپه	midnight.
شومه دم or شومه قلاَر	dead of night. 1 to 3 a.m.

149. The whole period of 24 hours is called شوا روز (=Persian شب و روز "night and day").

مال or مالي used after measures of time means *"about the time of."*

150. The foregoing subdivisions of day and night are those in common use, especially among uneducated Pathans. As, however, Pathans come more under European influence, they learn to use the divisions of the clock; e.g.—

يو بجه	one o'clock.
شپږ بجي	six o'clock.

This method necessitates the addition of سحر or دَ شپې to distinguish between day and night, thus :—

لس بجې سحر 10 a.m.
لس بجې دَ شپې 10 p.m.

151. It is important to bear in mind that the Mohammedan day begins at sunset, so that what we should call "Saturday night" must be rendered in Pushtu—

دَ اتوار په ورځ دَ شپې "Sunday" night

Unless this is remembered, much confusion will be the result when inquiring into the date of the occurrence of an event.

152. When speaking of the date on which an event happened, or is expected to happen, the following expressions are used :—

دَ دې مياشت "instant."
دَ تيرې مياشت "ultimo."
دَ بلې مياشت "proximo."

153. "What," referring to a date, takes the form of an Ordinal adjective: څويم, from څه "*what.*"

نن څويم تاريخ دې What is the date to-day?

GREETINGS.

154. The ordinary Pathan greetings are :—

(1) ستړې مه شې May you not be weary! (= Good day.)
(2) خوار مه شې } May you not be poor!
(3) مه خوارېږې }
(4) No. (1) joined with (2) or (3).

The reply to the greeting is :—

(1) تهٔ ستړي مهٔ شيَ May *you* not be weary ! (=Good day to *you*.)

(2) تهٔ خوار مهٔ شيَ } May *you* not be poor !
(3) تهٔ مهٔ خواريږې }

followed by خير دِ ويَ Is all well with you ?

When addressing a Pathan, these greetings should always be employed to open a conversation.

155. When taking leave of one another, one Pathan will say to the other :—

(1) پهٔ مخ دِ ښهٔ May good be before you ! (=Good luck to you !)

(2) خدائې دِ مل شه May God be your companion ! (=God be wi' ye =Good-bye.)

(3) خدائې دِ وساته May God keep you !

to which the other will reply :—

آمين تاسره The same to you !

156. When welcoming a guest to one's house, either of these two expressions can be used :—

پهٔ خير راغلې Welcome !
or
هر کله راشه Ever welcome !

COLLOQUIAL SENTENCES.

PAPERS SET AT HIGHER STANDARD PUSHTU EXAMINATIONS AT VARIOUS TIMES.

1873.

1. Call him in. What do you call this in Pushtu? Why did you call me? Is this place called Peshawar?

2. Cut this stick short. Bring the man before me. Take all these papers out of the basket. She gave birth to a child. Keep this goat till she brings forth a young one.

3. Come out of the room. He came up to me on the road. Climb over that wall. Attend to what I say.

4. He is killed. He was being beaten. Was he shot dead? Had he been with you, he would have also gone out shooting.

5. He came beating his drum. I beat you. A scorpion stung my toe. He beat him without a cause.

6. My watch has gone wrong. Have you made a wall round your premises? Have all my torn clothes repaired. Tell the carpenter to make a desk for me.

7. The fire is burning and blazing. See if the coal is burning. Do you smoke? Does he drink (liquor)? Burn the waste papers.

8. Just run this way. Just wait a bit. I have just arrived. Please turn towards me.

9. What is the time? What day of the month is it? What day of the week was yesterday? Come on this day week.

10. Read this line. Revise your yesterday's lesson. Learn these words by heart. Which is his to-day's writing? First spell the word and then say it.

11. Lie down. Is he asleep or awake? Who is lying down on the bed? What is lying there? Make him sleep.

12. Get up and don't sit by him. Who is sitting in the porch? Was he standing by the door? He stood quietly behind him.

13. Put the watch in front of me on this table and don't put it there! Who told you to put this thing here? Take care not to come by this road again. Have you arranged all my pictures?

14. I asked him to direct me to your place, but he did not do so. Show it to me. Have you shown it to him?

15. Let him go. Let them come. You can go. They have come. May I come? He has gone.

16. Take the box to the office. Who drove my carriage to the city? Will the herdsman take my cow to the pasture? Has the washerman taken away my dirty clothes?

17. Tie the horse to the tree. Untie it. How did the mule get loose? Wait. I waited for you yesterday. He has been waiting for an hour. Don't bother me. Don't be nervous. What do you mean? Do you understand what I mean? Please explain it to me.

18. Light the lamp. Take a match out of the box and strike it. A fire broke out at night and burnt a house to ashes. My hand has been burnt by a cigarette.

19. What have you done with my knife? What has become of him?

20. Open the door. Shut the window. Fasten the door back. Lock up the box. Open the chest. Open your Pushtu book and shut up this Urdu book. Open your eyes. Open your fingers and toes. Open your mouth. Hold your tongue. Shut your eyes. Spread a new carpet on my floor.

21. Brush my clothes and hang them all up on a peg. Put on your clothes, namely, a shirt, coat, hat, turban, gloves, waist-belt, and shoes.

22. What is it? What has happened? What is the matter? What is the matter with you?

23. Take either this or that. I would take neither. Which one do you like? I don't like either. I am thankful to you. He is much obliged to you.

24. When he had written the letter, he came to me. When you have written the letter, come to me.

25. If it had been in my power I would have taken you to Kabul. Had you come yesterday you would have seen me. If you had fired the gun, you would have killed the fox. If he had come I might have gone. Had I known him to be a thief, I would never have engaged him as my servant. Had he not given me leave, I would not have accompanied him. Had the police inspector not taken a bribe he would certainly have arrested the thieves.

1874.

1. Where have you come from? Do you know Amir Khan? How many sons has he? Are they by different mothers? Is his youngest son

stone-blind? What is the name of his fifth grandson? Is he a farmer or merely a farm labourer? Is his land watered by the rains only or irrigated by water-courses? How many wells and how many ploughs has he got?

2. Listen to what I say and answer my questions distinctly. Were you ever in the habit of staying in Abdulla's guest-house? When were you there last, and how long did you stay? Did you see an old woman there? Was her husband with her? Was he a boatman or a carpenter or a dyer? Was his paternal uncle there or his maternal uncle? I heard that his cousin was in the village at the time. Can you tell me any other circumstances that occurred that day? Have you any trustworthy witnesses who can swear that they saw you there?

3. Are you ready to start? His father will not let him read. He is a lazy boy and not much given to learning. He still reads in the mosque. He has finished reading the Qoran. The girls do not read. It is not the Pathan custom to teach girls. Their fathers will not allow them to read. Old men sometimes learn to read. You may go now. God be with you!

4. I will take it. He may take it. If you take it. He had thrown him. Let him wear it. I did not want it. Bring the dog. Bring the stick. Do not shout. The man was shearing the sheep. Have patience. Do not stir. Stay a little. Lift up this stone. Raise your arm. Stoop down. The day has passed Take off your shoes. Tie on your turban. Light the fire. I am not deaf.

5. I advise you not to keep the dog. He is mad and is of no use whatever. You perceive I merely desire your welfare. I am your friend and well-wisher. Who will prevent me? How many rupees do you require? Thirteen, sixteen or 23?

6. I have 5 buffaloes, 6 cows and 20 sheep. The horses are lame. The he-goats and the she-goats graze on the common. Your oxen are used in the ploughs. I have one donkey which has gone to the hills for firewood. I cannot afford to keep either a mule or a horse. There is no salt in our district. The Afridis bring it on camels from Kohat. If you start at once you will reach the village by the evening.

1875.

1. As the thief was digging into the wall of a dyer's house at midnight, the watchman came upon him. He at once fled, but left his jemmy by the hole. The Thanadar did his utmost but could not find any trace of him. It is said he took refuge with the Wazirs.

2. Why did you not raise the alarm, so that the villagers might have come to your assistance? Sir, I shouted several times, but no one came.

3. All plaintiff's witnesses have been bribed. Of this I feel assured. His

paternal uncle offered me a bribe to give false evidence; but I would not accept it.

4. If you have not got the leisure to prosecute your claim yourself, appoint an agent and give him a power-of-attorney.

5. When he had ploughed the field and sown the seed he went home.

6. Take care that every one gets his just dues and that there is no oppression of any kind.

7. The evidence of the witnesses is conflicting. This is the result of the factions which exist in the village. I do not believe that the accused really struck the deceased with his spade.

8. The Government demanded five hostages from the Mohmand Khels. They gave them, and the Commissioner sent them to the Lahore Jail.

9. If the woman had given her husband poison as you say, he must inevitably have died.

10. Every spring certain Afridi tribes appoint a rendezvous and migrate with their families to Tirah. There they spend the summer and come down to the plains in the autumn, and remain there during the winter.

11. Sir, I am afraid there will be a raid on my village this very night.

12. What did you do with the money which you received on the mortgage of your land? This prisoner pawned this silver necklace to a Hindu shopkeeper, and it has since been recognised as the minstrel's property.

13. When you found the corpse on the bank of the river, was there a rope around its neck?

14. The plaintiff sues for the custody of his wife, and enters in his petition the name of his mother-in-law as co-defendant. This man was always quarrelling with his wife and beating her, and therefore she would not live with him. He has now divorced her. Some influential persons have instigated the plaintiff to make a false claim.

15. I have no doubt but that the defendant really married the girl, and I credit the evidence of the old Mulla who deposes that he read the marriage service.

16. Sir, the fact is we filed a deed of compromise. Defendant will pay 10 rupees 8 annas per harvest. It is thus that we have settled the case at home. When the village headman arrested the prisoner and brought him to the police station, was he very much agitated in his manner or not?

17. There was no armed escort for safe conduct with the village cattle as they were grazing on the hills. A band of Wazirs came down and carried them off. The shepherds fled. The alarm drum was beaten in the village. The hue and cry party turned out in pursuit of the raiders and followed up their tracks as far as the Isa Khel ravine.

18. The Wazirs asked for ransom money, but the owners of the cattle would not give it. The Deputy Commissioner seized twenty camels of the Wazirs as reprisal. The Wazirs on this paid Rs. 550 as compensation to the owners, and Rs. 100 as a fine to Government.

19. The Malik's son was in love with my daughter, and she, five days ago, eloped with him across the border.

20. Sir, the girl was not Mahmud's wife, she was only his betrothed. As the accused's father has great influence in the village, Mahmud's father is willing to make peace with him, agreeably to Afghan custom. He will take either Rs. 250 as compensation or accused's eldest sister.

21. Barkat stabbed my son in the belly one watch before dawn, as he lay asleep in the Hujra. I accuse him of the murder. I suspect no one else. He is my enemy because a month ago a Jirga fined him Rs. 50 for having poisoned the buffalo which worked my Persian wheel well.

22. Defendant has broken down the boundary ridge between his field and mine and put a thorn hedge on my ancestral land. The jewels were found by a cowherd, buried in accused's field, and were dug up in the presence of the Thanadar.

23. The village barber's sheep are always trespassing in my jowar crop.

24. There were four bhusa stacks on my threshing floor. Some one set fire to them the day before yesterday after night prayers. If the accused and six of his relatives will swear on the Qoran to their innocence, I shall be satisfied and will withdraw my complaint.

25. The betrothal took place during the spring harvest. The father of the betrothed girl gave a feast to the whole village. I cannot understand why her brothers now deny that there was any betrothal. There must have been a betrothal: her brothers must be telling lies for some motive not known to you or me.

1878.

1. How long have you been learning Pushtu? If you study attentively the Pushtu idioms and carefully listen to the pronunciation, you will soon be able to speak the language so as to be understood.

2. The lightning struck the ship and set it on fire; the crew jumped into the sea and saved themselves by swimming.

3. Why did you not tell me that my father had arrived? He told me that he was coming to see me.

4. Take care that the enemy do not surround you.

5. This year, on account of scarcity of rain, there is little grass in the district. I fear there will be a famine.

6. Who called me? Send for some labourers (forced).

7. This man is very tall and that woman is very short.

8. This grass is green. These bulls are very fat.

9. How much water is there in this well? Is the river fordable, or do the people cross in boats? Can a person cross by swimming?

10. Why did you laugh? Why did you weep? Have you bathed?

11. Make that man get upon the roof of the house, that he may view the country all around the village.

12. I saw a man running with a drawn sword in his hand.

13. How far is it from here to Peshawar? Does the road lead straight to the city?

14. If he should come, what would you do?

15. I am hungry, thirsty and tired. Let me lie down.

16. The horse stumbled and fell.

17. What hour has just struck?

18. The Pathans got possession of the pass and fought desperately. Can laden camels cross the hills by this pass? Is it very steep? Is the way stony or is there a well marked road? The hill was so steep that neither mules nor horses could ascend it.

19. Are those goats grazing on that cliff?

20. Divide the money among these men. Give two rupees to each man. If they work for the whole day I will increase their wages.

21. Close all the doors, a dust storm has come.

22. If the man had been well beaten at first, he would not have committed this crime. He knocked me down but I struck him on the head. I gave him a wound with my sword and the blood flowed copiously. He did not heed the wound but fiercely attacked me. Never before was there such a severe fight, now they are at peace among themselves.

23. Do not get confused; speak plainly and to the point. Why are you trembling?

24. The sun rises in the East and sets in the West.

25. He scatters seed. This is very poor land and that is very good. There is no rope to this well. This land is very sandy. Who has ploughed this land? How many ploughmen have you got? The lambardar's plough oxen are very old and thin.

April 1883.

1. Take away this man. Bring the cow.

2. I did not strike him. He struck me. My enemy cut me on the right shoulder with a sword.

3. Why hast thou come? Come inside. Welcome.

4. I may have opened it. You are not as tall as he is. There is danger on this road at night.

5. These are good women. This man contends with me. He is an unfortunate man. Why so? Five of his cattle died last week from some disease or other.

6. I went alone. Catch the thieves. He enticed him away.

7. How many stacks of straw are there in the village? Give the labourers five loaves each. The five men must meet me in the city at noon to-morrow. He says there are not two sisters but one. I know that there are two. I have heard that there are nine goats in the village. There is not enough for all of us, but you can take half.

8. Hire a camel for me. Unload the mule. Unload these carts. What weight does a mule carry? A camel carries five maunds.

9. This man has a great idea of himself. If he had not enlisted as a Government servant he would have been a general in Kabul, because he can read and write well.

10. The horse jumps very well. It is not a horse; it is a colt.

11. There are eleven witnesses on his side, but three of them have sworn falsely. They will be apprehended. I suppose they have been bribed. Yes, a man cannot take a bribe and tell the truth too.

12. One day a wolf seized a sheep by its neck.

13. The boy used to bathe in the river.

14. Why do you blame him?

15. Why is there this strife amongst yourselves? We quarrel about our turn for water.

16. Has this field no ridge? It had, but it has fallen down.

October 1884.

1. Its hair is black, its face is white, its tail is not very long.

2. It happened too that the heat of this year was uncommonly oppressive.

3. The camels stuck in the snow.

4. The water-courses are small.

5. The jungle is full of animals.

6. He started from the village at daybreak.

7. Go and reap that wheat.

8. Why did he hit you?

9. They slaughtered a goat.

10. If they arrive late, give them bread.

11. The regiment intends marching to-morrow. Select a good site for the camp. Ask the Malik of the village to be present.

12. What crops have you in your village? Mention a few of them.

13. Is there any river near your village? Are the lands irrigated by cuts from streams or from wells?

14. What shares do the tenants pay to the owners of land from the crops?

15. Have there been any robberies in your village? The thieves generally come when all is still.

16. The chowkidar reported the matter at the police station. The headman's house has been broken into from the west. The deputy inspector came to make enquiries.

17. The cultivator gives a quarter of the produce of his wheat, barley, dal and mustard to the owner and half of his rice and sugar-cane.

18. The Khan's mill is broken. We are forced to go a long way to have our grain ground. Women usually carry the sacks.

19. There was an eclipse of the sun the other day which was visible from Peshawar.

20. A flood in Bara carried the dam away; the Kaleels and Mohmands have gone to repair it.

21. What is the price of your bhusa stacks? Sell it to me cheap, I am poor.

22. Where lies the ford? How is it crossed? By raft or by a regular ferry?

23. We collect skins and prepare a raft when necessary. There is no ferry. We are generally fired at when we cross the stream.

24. Tell the Subadar to see the sentries at 10 P.M., at 2 A.M., and just before dawn. This is a famous place for thieves.

25. This has been a year of great scarcity. Little rain has fallen. The earthquakes have been many.

October 1885.

1. Is there any good grazing ground for camels near Cantonments? Three of the mules have sore backs and must not be laden. This mare has been lame since last Ramzan.

2. Is there any danger in shooting on those hills? Am I likely to find wildfowl on the river?

3. The wheat and barley harvests have been very good this year. Tell me the approximate revenue got from irrigated and unirrigated land in your village.

4. Show me the nearest road to my camp. If you really had presented a petition I would have heard it at once. Is it likely that the common people in your village will listen to the advice of the elders?

5. The watchman says that when he first saw the thieves, they were just leaving the bunniah's shop. It will, I think, be better for you to explain the whole circumstances exactly as they occurred. You will gain nothing by telling a falsehood.

6. My family has had a blood-feud with Bairam's family for many years. The whole tribe has been blockaded on account of a raid committed three years ago.

7. What medicine do your doctors administer in the case of fever? He has been a cripple since his birth. Speak slowly; I shall then understand all you say.

8. When do you think the river will be in flood? How many men have been captured? Bring them all before me. Are there any water-mills near the village or are hand-mills generally used?

9. Tell the Subadar to choose a naik and five sturdy sepoys and post them in the ravine to the rear of the camp. By how many days has this sepoy overstayed his leave?

10. Any Khan who brings twenty men with their horses for service in the regiment will receive a Jemadar's commission. I notice that the horses of those men who have just rejoined from leave are in very poor condition. You will be pleased to hear that this is the last question which will be put to you.

April 1886.

1. What supplies are procurable from Peshawar to Chamkanni? We want rice, barley, wheat and grass.

2. Has it been raining? Are the roads good? Tell the bunniahs to have everything ready.

3. The regiment will march at 5 A.M. The men should take some food with them.

4. Is there any river on the road? How can it be crossed? By a bridge, boat or ford?

5. Is that a pomegranate tree? No, it is a mulberry: the fruit will ripen soon.

6. My brother is the Khan of that village; the lambardar is named Akbar, and Khawas is the chowkidar.

7. A flood came down the Kabul river. Nowshera was carried away, the guest-house of Rahmat only remained.

8. Rain is good for the country. The floods have destroyed all the crops. The Indian corn is entirely ruined.

9. Who are you? What do you want? I have come to make a report as I am the chowkidar of Peshawar. There was a burglary at the house of Sultan last night.

10. The attempt was made from the rear of the house. The residents were awake, the police alert, all the offenders have been arrested. Well done!

11. Is there any shooting on the banks of the river?

12. Have the quail come in yet?

13. You people generally prefer hawking to shooting.

14. I like the look of this horse very much, but he appears to be lame.

15. Government has demanded hostages from the tribe.

16. If they agree to Government terms there will not be an expedition against them.

17. If they commit raids we will make reprisals.

18. Is there much crime in your village?

19. Four men were convicted of murder yesterday and sentenced to death.

20. One man escaped to Independent Territory.

October 1886.

1. The village cattle were driven to the grazing ground at daybreak.

2. The river rises in the heart of the hills and its spring is said to be as cold as ice.

3. Fish are caught at Nisatta in large numbers. They are brought into Cantonments and sold at remunerative prices.

4. The city is populous and the roads and lanes are narrow and ill kept.

5. Every kind of sport is procurable here but the inhabitants prefer to take their ease at home.

6. Order a Native Officer to go on ahead and arrange for supplies.

7. Take 100 sowars with you and make a sketch of the country.

8. Heavy firing was maintained on both wings till nightfall.

9. The regiment is to be armed with lances instead of with sabres.

10. The enemy fled helter-skelter down the hill as soon as our guns opened fire.

11. Say concisely how the affair occurred and merely say what you saw yourself, not what you heard from others.

12. When you first saw the accused, was he coming towards his house or had he arrived there?

13. If you were on the spot when the murder occurred, as you have

stated, you must have noticed whether there was anyone else there, besides the prisoner and the murdered man.

14. If you had given notice to the Thanadar of the enmity which existed between the parties, he would have made arrangements to prevent crime.

15. The night was very dark and there was no moon; how then can you describe exactly what clothes the man was wearing?

16. Put out your tongue. You must take this medicine at once, otherwise the fever will recur.

17. Unless you allow me to cut off your leg you will never recover.

18. Do you cultivate any autumn crops on irrigated lands?

19. There has been very little rain since the spring, but the heavy snow which fell in the winter has caused a plentiful supply of water in the Bara river, consequently the irrigated land has not suffered.

20. We have sown some of the Indian corn seed which you gave us. The grain is very good, but the stalks are so hard that the cattle will not eat them.

April 1887.

1. What is the name of that ravine? Where does it come from? It runs from Laka Sar to the Kabul river.

2. Is there ever any water in it? Yes, when the snow melts in the hills a great deal of water comes down and we build dams across the ravine and take the water off to irrigate the fields.

3. What is the condition of your crops this year? What crops do you sow? Do you make most money out of the spring or autumn harvest? I hear rats often get into the corn-stacks; do they cause much damage, and how do you get them out?

4. I am going to Matanni to-morrow morning. Take my black horse to the chauki near the Bara bridge, and post the mare at Badaber. You start to-night and I shall leave at 6 o'clock in the morning.

5. Is there any sport in the district? Yes, there are several large jheels in which numbers of snipe are found and also teal. On the river there are any amount of duck and large flocks of sand grouse on the open plains.

6. I am going out shooting this afternoon but will not take you or the dogs with me. Keep them here till I return; don't take them away.

7. My regiment starts for Cherat on the 28th. You go on the day before and see that all necessary supplies are collected. The Tahsildar will help you.

8. Be very careful that the lambardars of the village supply you with

good chowkidars and take none but men of good character. It is a bad place and we can't be too careful.

9. Has there been much crime in your village lately? Yes, last month there were three burglaries, one murder, and several thefts. A drought occurred this year, and the bad characters, being hard up, turned their hands to stealing.

10. A case occurred ten days ago in which a lambardar carried off Amir's wife. The police came and enquired into the matter, but the deputy inspector took a bribe and let the offender off. The woman had been sold for Rs. 200 to a chief in Independent Territory, and her husband had to ransom her.

11. How is the river crossed? Is it fordable or is there a ferry boat? Is the boat pulled across by a rope or is it rowed? How deep is the river?

12. A flood came down last year just as a boat full of women was crossing. The rope broke, the boat was washed away, caught in a whirlpool, upset and all the women were drowned. The boatmen, however, who could swim got to the shore safe.

October 1887.

1. I say, Khan, what is the news of your village? Is all well there? Are the crops good and plentiful? Have you had any crime within the last month?

2. The only news of any importance is that everything is very dear. We are having famine rates. There has been no rain. The well crops have been eaten up by rats. The only people who have flourished are the thieves.

3. What description of lands have you in your village? Are they irrigated by water-cuts from the river or from wells, or are your crops dependent on the rainfall?

4. Our lands are all dependent on rainfall. In former years the water was brought from the river by a canal; but the channel has been filled up and the people are too lazy to clear it out.

5. If our lands were all irrigated from the river, or from wells, we should not suffer as we do. Then there would be no bad harvests and the revenue would be paid without difficulty.

6. Trust in God and His prophet. Next year the crops of barley, wheat, mustard, millet, Indian corn, rice and sugar-cane, will be excellent. Then no one will complain and all will be contented.

7. What is the name of that village? Who are the lambardars? Are there two or more? How many watchmen? Is there any guest-house and who owns it?

8. The name of the village is Shalbandi. The lambardars are two in number. They are friends with all the thieves in the neighbourhood and in these days of pleaders they have a nice time of it.

9. Are there no means of punishing them for their misdeeds? Yes, there are, but it is very hard to bring their offences home to them. All the bad characters are on their side.

10. The crimes are generally thus committed. All the men of each village attend at the guest-houses. The women alone sleep in their houses. When all is still an attempt is made to break into a place.

11. In the morning a report is made at the police station. The deputy inspector arrives with his constables. There is a great stir made; but the lambardars ruin every case.

12. What is the name of that river? How is it crossed? Is there any ford, ferry or bridge for the use of travellers?

13. It is a bad stream and very narrow, with steep banks. There is seldom any water in it; but if it rains in a particular locality down comes the flood.

14. It then carries away everything before it. Last year one mosque went; the year before Ismail's house was carried away. Now it may be someone else's chance to suffer.

15. What sort of road have you from here to Pabbi? Are there trees on either side?

16. Are the encamping grounds clean? Are supplies obtainable? They will be wanted for troops going to Cherat.

17. Yes, the bunniahs have been ordered to provide everything. Owing to the severe frosts grass will be difficult to procure.

18. The regiment will be inspected to-morrow at five in the morning. The General is very particular. Take care that the musketry returns are all correct.

19. We shall be quite prepared for him. Our men are splendid shots, and have been carefully instructed in what they are to do.

20. A boat full of pilgrims was going down the river. Getting caught in a whirlpool the rudder broke, the boat was upset and all were drowned.

April 1888.

1. Have you seen the Khan? What news has he to give? Has there been any rain? The Khan said it had fallen at the proper time.

2. There was no danger in cutting wood. The bunniahs were unhappy as they had been collecting grain.

3. Our village crops are barley, wheat and mustard in the spring. Later

on we grow rice, Indian corn and sugar-cane. Rats have been very troublesome this year.

4. Is there much water in the Swat canal? I hear it commences near Abázai and goes towards Mardan.

5. The Khan is becoming very wealthy. Last year some of the Zemindars would not take water from the canal. They expected rain but none fell.

6. The entrance to the village is from the north; you pass between the two towers. A little to the right lies the guest-house of the Khan. Further on to the left is the musjid of Omar. The Khan is very friendly with the thieves. He keeps two chowkidars; they steal from the villagers and send the property across the border. The Khan gets his share.

7. What do the police do? The thanadar comes and asks the headman. They tell a story of their own and implicate border men. This relieves the police of further trouble. This is a regular Pathan custom.

8. I wish to go to Abazai. What road must I take? Are there any bridges? No, there are none. You must search for fords on both rivers.

9. The Swat river comes down by Abazai. The Kabul river flows by Michni. Both unite some distance from Nowshera.

10. The Kaka Khels bring lots of wood (logs) down the river. This year they are very unhappy: all their timber has been seized by a tyrannical ruler.

11. The regiment is ordered to Cherat. It will march on Saturday. What sort of road is it? The road is very good. There are trees on either side with clumps here and there.

12. The quartermaster must see to the tents. Bunniahs will have supplies at every halting-ground. We shall march stage by stage. The regiment will be inspected by the General. Everything must be ready by 6 A.M. The Adjutant gives a lot of trouble at these parades. Never mind musketry, our men are good shots. We shall do well.

13. There have been few pilgrims this year from Bokhara. They go now by the Russian railway. Travelling in Afghanistan is very troublesome.

14. How do you go to Dir? The road leads through Mardan over the Malakand Pass into Swat. The people there are very simple. The Mullas mislead the people, though some are very good. They advise them to speak the truth, be kind to the poor and commit no murder.

15. Has the revenue been collected this year? The tahsildars have been very busy. The wealthy Arbabs and Zamindars are the last to pay in their instalments.

October 1888.

1. Who is the Khan of this village? Is he a wealthy man? Has he lots of land? What revenue does he pay to Government?

2. The Khan's name is Akbar Khan. He has an income of Rs. 2,000 a year. This enables him to keep up a guest-house. He pays Rs. 50 half-yearly as revenue.

3. His village is situated on the other bank of the Lunda river. This side is very steep. Even if a flood comes down his place never suffers. A small garden supplies him with apples, grapes and quinces.

4. His irrigated lands provide him with wheat, barley, mustard, rice, sugar-cane and cotton. He is a good landlord and liked by his tenants.

5. Did you see any game as you rode from Mattra yesterday? No, I did not. I heard the quails are in. I saw several call-birds out in the fields.

6. The shikari tells me that snipe and duck and geese are in. He saw snipe in the Shahi jheel and duck and geese on the Kabul river.

7. The shooting here is very poor and hard work with a large garrison here. Numbers of soldiers are out every day. The birds in time get very wild and you are very lucky if you can get six in as many hours.

8. Which road do you generally take? I ride down the artillery parade and cross by the ford. Look out for the quicksand if you follow this line.

9. On the river by Daodzai there is a bridge; lower down there is a boat which is pulled to either bank by a rope.

10. What crime in this district is on the increase?

11. In a blood-feud how are matters managed?

12. Akbar Khan's stacks were burnt; he had Mowaz Khan's cattle poisoned. Mowaz then had Akbar Khan's trees destroyed.

13. Last night there was an alarm in our village. It was in the eastern quarter. A man had broken into a house and alarmed the inmates.

14. The owner fired his pistol at the thief. The thief escaped into the courtyard, ran up the steps to the top of the house and then jumped down into the lane. He then went into the masjid and lay down.

15. The regiment will march on Saturday for the Agror campaign. It will be inspected by the General on Friday. See that everything is ready and complete.

16. It will march stage by stage to Darband. Is the carriage all provided? How many camels, mules, ponies and carts have been told off to us?

17. The bunniahs must have all supplies ready; they will be wanted at every camping-ground. They must have milk.

18. From Darband the road is very difficult; it leads up the left bank of the Indus to the Kot Kai. Ravines and precipices have to be faced.

19. Our cause is just and we shall win. The enemy has already suffered much and the fanatics are going away.

20. Five boats have been collected. Tell the boatmen to collect more and remain ready.

April 1889.

1. Call that man here. Ask him his name and from what village he comes. Where is his house?

2. My name is Akbar. I live at Sufaid Dheri and my house is just behind the mosque.

3. What lands have you got? They are *abi*, and the water supply comes from the Bara river. The dam is all right this year.

4. The usual crops are wheat, barley, mustard, rice, sugar-cane and cotton. In autumn we have Indian corn.

5. The revenue is not heavy, the people are very poor. They spend all their money in civil and criminal suits.

6. Is there a guest-house in that village? Yes, and it belongs to Ṣikandar Khan. He is a good landlord and liked by all.

7. The people are very ignorant. They are quarrelsome also. Bitter feuds prevail amongst them and this leads to murder.

8. I went to Daodzai. The river had to be crossed twice. At one place there was a bridge, at the other a boat which was pulled from bank to bank by a rope.

9. The police have hard work here. Theft, housebreaking and murder are the chief offences. The prison is full of prisoners.

10. All was quiet in the *Kandi*. An alarm was suddenly raised. The chowkidar came to enquire.

11. The house of Jumma Khan had been entered. The thief ascended the wall by a ladder. He then jumped into the courtyard.

12. What bird is that? People call it a quail. Are they in now?

13. Yes, they are. Send out call-birds. You may get twenty to thirty every morning.

14. Snipe and duck are very scarce, but lots of bustard have come in this winter.

15. I am fond of shikar but can spare no time to get out.

16. Have any orders come for the regiment? Yes, we march on Saturday. See that everything is ready.

17. The camels and mules should be sent for. The tents are all repaired.

18. How many bunniahs are there? One to each company. They must have all supplies ready.

19. The General saw the regiment. The firing has been good. The men are young and strong.

20. Is this place called Taru Jabba? It is famous for thieves. Warn the night sentries to load with buckshot cartridges.

October 1889.

1. Is there much water in the Kabul river? No, the stream is very low. Little snow fell on the Sufaid Koh during the last winter.

2. Is the water supply due entirely to rains and snow? Are there no springs on the river bank? What is the depth of the water in the river between Warsak and Michni?

3. How do you cross between Dakka and Lalpura? By ford, bridge, boat or raft? Chiefly by boat, which is moved by a rope tied to either bank.

4. I see that you have rafts and inflated skins on this river. The boatmen use an oar in place of a regular rudder. The custom, though universal, is not perfect.

5. A raft of wood was being sent down stream. It first stuck on a sandbank which turned out to be a quicksand. Later on it came into a whirlpool and all the occupants were drowned.

6. It is proposed to make a canal from near Warsak. The lands at the head of the cut will get most water. The country can produce wheat, barley, grain, millet, Indian corn, sugar-cane, cotton and mustard.

7. How is the revenue fixed in this village and calculated? One-third on land irrigated from the canal and one-tenth on unirrigated land. It is light.

8. Whose house is that? Ibrahim Khan's. It is built of lime and pakka bricks. There is an under-room for the hot weather.

9. To reach this house you first enter the village. The gate has one tower over it, with stone steps to the top of the roof.

10. Then comes the masjid with its pretty tank, its garden filled with mulberry, almond and peach trees. The Mullas eat all the fruit.

11. Has the Khan a guest-house? He has two. He is famous for his hospitality. This has brought him into debt.

12. That fat man is the Khan's enemy. He has bribed all the police and Tahsil officials, who make up cases against the Khan.

13. Last night about 10 P.M. I was going along the alley. Everything

was still. Suddenly I heard a shot in the southern quarter. I stood still to listen.

14. The chowkidar came running along. He said that a burglary had been attempted on a certain house. He did not know the owner's name.

15. The thief stole into the courtyard. In making a hole he roused the husband, whose wife shrieked. The man then bolted.

16. He rushed up the staircase to the roof, jumped into the street, and fled to the masjid. People suspect that he is probably a seeker after knowledge.

17. I went to shoot in the Tartarra Range a week ago. We saw a couple of markhor and one urial.

18. In going up hill I stumbled and fell down. A stone rolled down and went into the river. This frightened the animals who ran away.

19. What sport have you in this district? There are snipe, duck, bustard, wild goose, swan and quail. Now and then you see a hare or deer.

20. The regiment will march at 6 A.M. Have everything ready. The bunniahs must have supplies.

April 1890.

1. Who is that man? He is a Zamindar in the village of Tangi. He is the owner of 2,000 jaribs of unirrigated land.

2. How are his irrigated lands watered? By a cut from the Swat river The lands at the head of the cut get the most water. Yes, this is true.

3. His revenue is thus fixed. The irrigated lands pay half the produce. The rest are assessed at one-tenth. His revenue is light.

4. He has two guest-houses. He has built a mosque. He is noted for his hospitality. The searchers after knowledge resort to his mosque. They are a very bad lot.

5. The lands produce wheat, barley, clover, mustard, cotton, sugar-cane, Indian corn and millet. The value of a jarib of sugar-cane is sometimes as much as 60 rupees.

6. What sport have you in this district? Not much in the way of deer but there are lots of birds: There are quail, partridge, chikor, snipe, duck, bustard and goose.

7. I went to shoot in the Shahi jheel. I got six brace of snipe. The birds were very wild and had been frightened by the village cattle.

8. I saw some geese also, but they would not let me come near them. The day was cloudy with slight rain and no sun at all.

9. Do you ever see deer here? No, they have all been driven away. Sometimes urial and markhor are to be found in the hills.

10. Take care how you cross that river. Is there a ford? Look out for the quicksands. Possibly there is a ferry or a bridge or a boat pulled from bank to bank by a rope.

11. Last year a flood came down the Kabul river. Two water-mills were carried away. Three quarters or sections of the village of Nowshera were under water. A boat with ten boatmen sank in the whirlpool.

12. What is the condition of crime in Peshawar? . Very bad indeed. Two constables were wounded one night outside the city and their arms were taken away.

13. Who were the offenders? This matter is not known yet. Some say it was done by Mohmands; others say it was the act of outlaws amongst the Kuki Khels. A third report lays the blame on the Udi Khels of Laghman.

14. The village was perfectly still as I went to my house. It was the hour of midnight. As I got close to Ibrahim Khan's house I heard a shot fired in the southern quarter of the village.

15. The chowkidars came running fast to me. I asked what had happened. They said that Khuaja's house had been broken into. He was roused and ran, but still the thieves fired a shot at him.

16. How did the thieves escape? They ran into the courtyard, got up by the stairs to the top of the house, then down; by the vine into the lane and hid in the mosque.

17. The regiment will be inspected by the General. The parade will be at 6 A.M. Be careful about your musketry. Our march commences on Saturday next.

18. Are the tents all ready? What number of mules and camels will be required? 300 mules and 400 camels.

19. Supplies of all sorts will be wanted at each stage, especially bhoosa and gram. Tell the bunniahs to go on and make all arrangements in time.

20. Taru is a bad place for thieves. Nowshera, Akora and Khyrabad are equally so. The chowkidars are thieves and no trust can be placed in them.

October 1890.

1. Who are you? What is you name? What is your occupation? Are you a landowner, cultivator or trader? What is your income every year?

2. I am a cultivator and live in Yusufzai. I cultivate ten jaribs of land and give my landlord one-third of the produce. He is a great tyrant and ruins all his tenants.

3. Why don't you complain to Government against him? What would be the use? He has bribed the chowkidars, headmen, chuprasis, Tahsildar and all are in his pay.

4. My lands lie close to the canal. I get the first supply, but even then my crops have failed this year. Everyone hates this landlord who fattens on his cultivators.

5. Our spring crops are wheat and barley. In the autumn we have Indian corn, sugar-cane and cotton. This land also produces millet, mustard, gram, radishes, turnips and carrots.

6. The village lands are both irrigated and unirrigated. On the former we pay 2 rupees a jarib and a water tax of 4. On the latter we hand over one-tenth of the produce to the owner. The revenue is not heavy and we ought to be rich.

7. I started last night for Michni. On the road I met a lot of Mohmands coming with convoys to Peshawar. There was no ford or bridge on the Kabul river. People were taken from bank to bank in a boat pulled across by a rope.

8. Whose house is that? It is Khuaja's house, where his father fed guests. He would never give a piece of bread to anyone. All the people dislike him very much. He is stout and a miser.

9. The flood came down the river. At what hour was it? The people were just then going to the mosque. Mohabat Khan's mosque is famous in all Peshawar.

10. Can you direct me to Taikal? Yes, go straight down that road and take the first turn to the left. One *kos* farther on you will see a white building. It belongs to Fateh Khan.

11. I took a boat and went down the river. We had four boatmen and two oars. A flood came down and broke the rudder. Two men were drowned.

12. What is the name of that jheel? It belongs to Shahi village. There are snipe, bustard, duck, geese and swans to be shot at. Quail come in later and are very scarce now.

13. I had two shots and missed both birds. Such is my fate. The powder was damp. The caps (gun) are very bad.

14. It was a moonlight night. All was still in the village as I went along the alley. Look out! What is that cry? I heard a shot fired.

15. The cry was in the eastern quarter of the village. The chowkidar came running along and I asked what was the matter. He was greatly alarmed.

16. He said that a burglary had been committed. The thieves got into the courtyard and dug below the foundation. The noise alarmed the owner.

17. He fired a pistol at the thief. It hit him in the right hand. The thief ran up the staircase, ascended the roof and jumped into the lane and hid in the musjid.

18. They asked the Mulla. He said that the thief was a searcher after knowledge. They are always giving trouble.

19. The deputy inspector came and wanted a bribe of 100 rupees. Why did he want so much? To hush up the case.

20. The regiment will march to-morrow. Get supplies ready at every stage. Warn the bunniahs.

November 1890.

(Special Examination held at Abbottabad.)

1. How many armed men are there in your village?
2. About twenty not counting the old men.
3. Tell the Subadar that the escort will march to-morrow at dawn, halting by the mosque at Peshawar.
4. Will the men go fully equipped?
5. Yes, and they will carry forty rounds of ball cartridge each.
6. The bhisties will march at the same time and fill their water-skins before starting as the road lies through a desert.
7. To-day a havildar of a Frontier regiment asked for leave to carry a sword and pistol across the border, as he was engaged in a blood-feud and expected to be attacked by his enemy.
8. Do you think that the crops of this year have been injured by the drought or has the canal saved them?
9. I was badly wounded in the thigh and have been lame ever since.
10. Do you think that hostages should be taken from the tribes on the frontier of Hazara?
11. Be careful in passing the water-mill, as spies say that an ambush has been laid there by the enemy.
12. The barrels of the rifles should not be allowed to glitter and without doubt you will surprise them.
13. Go down the river on the left and keep well hidden.
14. My horse is in poor condition; tell the syce to give it more grass.
15. What kind of sport do you get in the hills round?
16. There are hare and a few wild goats but jackals play havoc with the birds.
17. Pitch my tent by the stream in front of the village and you can then go to the guest-house.
18. A deputation has just come in from the Khyber chiefs who wish to ransom the hostages.
19. Very well, tell them that a ransom of Rs. 10,000 will be taken if paid in cash.
20. Do you think that the Persian wheel is a good way to irrigate land?

April 1891.

1. You say there has been no rain. It has been raining and snowing for the last three months. How are the crops?

2. The chances of wheat, barley, mustard, dal and clover are very good. Later on there will be Indian corn, millet and cotton. Of this we know nothing at present.

3. Who is that fat man? He is the Khan of Hoti. He is owner of 10,000 jaribs of irrigated and 15,000 of unirrigated land.

4. What revenue does he pay? For lands at the head of the stream 5 rupees an acre. For the other 2 annas a jarib.

5. His village is situated on the left bank of the stream. He has two mosques and three guest-houses. But no one gets any food out of him.

6. Is there any sport to be had? What game is to be found in Peshawar? Snipe, duck, geese; later on the quail come in. In the *maira* bustard and sand grouse are to be found.

7. What is the name of this village? Who is the Khan? Is he known for his hospitality?

8. I want to go to Taru. Which is the road? How can I get there? By the river or by rail.

9. Why do you wish to go there? Because a lot of offences have been committed there. It is a bad village.

10. Two nights ago there was a burglary. It was a cold still night. A shot was heard in the eastern quarter. The chowkidar ran in that direction.

11. The Khan's house had been broken into and a hole made in the south wall. The noise had roused the master, who fired at the thief.

12. Who was the thief? I can't well say. He must have been a seeker after knowledge.

13. The man went up the stairs, reached the top of the house, jumped into the lane, and fled to the mosque.

14. The deputy inspector came to make enquiries. He is a very long-headed fellow. He immediately reported that the thief came from across the border.

15. But why did he do this? Because once you bring in the trans-border people, the case is transferred to the political file.

16. In crossing that river look out for the bridge. If there is no bridge, examine the ford or go to the boat, which is pulled from bank to bank by a rope.

17. I rode my horse down the right bank. I found it full of quicksands and quagmires. It was very dangerous.

18. The General will inspect the regiment to-morrow. See that everything is ready; all the tents repaired, and the bunniahs' accounts settled.

19. The regiment starts for the Black Mountain at 5 A.M. Supplies must be got at every station. Warn the bunniahs of this.

20. A boat full of pilgrims went down the river. Came to a whirlpool. The oars and rudder were broken. All the men were drowned.

October 1891.

1. Take the recruits to the range at 5 o'clock and have everything ready there. Take down with you ten rounds for each man.

2. Subadar, I have sent for you about the theft of those rifles. I suspect that man who was enlisted last week.

3. I have made enquiries and have found out that his uncle, a well-known bad character, was in the city yesterday; but I do not believe the rifles have crossed the border yet.

4. Now, then, be quick. Get those loads off the camels. Divide them and put them on the mules. At this rate we sha'n't be across the Pass by sunset.

5. Take the horse to the house. Tell my servant to come here and bring my gun with him.

6. There is very little sport in my country. The hills are very steep and roads bad. There are also three streams which must be crossed.

7. I have heard that there are plenty of chikor and black partridge there, and that occasionally some markhor come down from the hills. The truth is you do not want me to come.

8. I am willing myself to take you all over the country and be responsible for your safety.

9. Malik, this is a bad business about this raid. If you can't keep your people in order Government will have to take other measures to stop their raiding. Remember, until this is satisfactorily settled, the tribal allowances as well as your own are stopped.

10. Sahib, what can I do? They won't obey me. The best way is to make reprisals on them when they bring their families down in the winter.

11. Raiders may try and drive off the cattle to-night. Try and arrange an ambush for them.

12. This year the locusts did much damage to the fruit trees, especially to the orange, peach and pear trees, and also to the wild grapes. The wheat and barley crops escaped.

13. This is the third murder in that village due to this blood-feud.

This one was committed in broad daylight. It is a clear case for a heavy fine on the whole village.

14. Was no clue discovered in that last case?

15. Well, sahib, there was no evidence; but one of the villagers absconded the same night, so no doubt he is guilty.

April 1892.

1. Who is that man? What is he doing? Where does he come from? What is his occupation?

2. His name is Ahmad. By trade he is a fisherman. He lives at Tangi and is the owner of one boat.

3. He catches fish in the Swat river. These he brings to sell in the city of Peshawar. His trade is flourishing.

4. Where is Abazai? It is about 30 miles from Peshawar city. The Swat canal commences in that quarter. In 1876 a lot of coolies were killed there.

5. What occurred then? The Sarkar sent troops to punish the Utman Khels. The Guides seized Sapri. The Utman Khels had to pay a fine of Rs. 5,000.

6. Yesterday I was coming along the Shahi jheel. I saw snipe, duck and goose. The birds were very wild. What did you shoot?

7. I had my gun and got five snipe, six duck and three geese. The cattle were in the jheel and they frightened the birds.

8. What season of the year is it? In two months it will be spring. The quail will then be in. Have your call-birds ready.

9. What grows here? Barley, wheat and mustard. The bustard are very fond of mustard. In the autumn we have sugar-cane.

10. What land have you got? Ten jaribs of irrigated and fifty of unirrigated land. The irrigated land I plough myself but the other I give to cultivators.

11. I pay Government 10 rupees a year for my irrigated lands. This as revenue and 2 rupees a year revenue for the rest.

12. Has there been any rain? Yes, but very little. My lands lie close to the canal. On this account I manage very well.

13. This is a bad village. It is famous for thieves. Last year a hundred cases were committed here. Only ten were proved.

14. How was this? The lambardars keep a number of thieves. They have friends across the border. These come and commit offences.

15. What follows then? The property is taken to Akhor and kept there. Other men are charged, who escape. The police all take bribes.

16. Last night, when all was still, a burglary was committed in Ahmed's house. He complained against his enemy Akbar. In truth the thief was a searcher after knowledge.

17. The thief got into the courtyard. He broke the door. The noise roused the owner. The man then fled to the mosque which lies in the eastern quarter of the village.

18. Have any orders been received for the regiment? Yes, it will be inspected to-morrow, and march on Friday for Cherat.

19. Ask the quartermaster to have the tents repaired and warn the bunniahs to have supplies ready at every stage. The milk must be fresh and good.

20. On arrival at Taru warn the police and headmen. They must have chowkidars round the camp. Sentries should be watchful and on the alert.

October 1892.

1. I want to see Toru. The village lies close to the Kalpani ravine. Do you know the plain?

2. Yes, I do. The Khan is named Mohabat Khan. He has a brother and two sons. He is famous for his hospitality.

3. He has two guest-houses and a mosque where all the people come to say prayers on Friday. His mulla is a friend of the Manki mulla.

4. What lands has the Khan got? Two thousand jaribs of unirrigated and one thousand of irrigated lands. The Swat river canal flows by Toru.

5. What revenue does he pay yearly? Two thousand rupees each harvest. The crops are wheat, barley, mustard and Indian corn.

6. Who is that stout Khan? He comes from the Mardan Taksil. His cultivators call him a great tyrant.

7. What game is there in the country? Snipe, duck and obara; but they all go away during the spring.

8. What are those hills? People call them the Pajja mountains. Beyond this lies the Buner country. Hashim Ali Khan is there.

9. Seesi and chikor are plentiful there. You must be up early to shoot them. They go away when the village cattle come out.

10. I went yesterday to the Shahi jheel. It was very dry and full of high grass. I shot only five snipe.

11. Is that man a thief? Yes, a notorious one. He has been convicted seven times and suffered twenty years' imprisonment.

12. Does he like imprisonment? Yes, he says the superintendent is very kind, and he obtains his medicine and food free. The jailor has a tender regard for thieves.

13. Sometimes a thief tells the jailor, "I will be free to-morrow and return in ten days; keep my corner ready for me."

14. It was all still in the village. All the people and dogs were sleeping. A shot was fired in the southern quarter of the village.

15. The chowkidar came running along the alley. He saw a man standing near the mosque. Hearing steps this man fled towards the river.

16. It being a moonlight night, the man jumped into a boat, seized the oar and in this way reached the other bank.

17. The regiment will be inspected to-morrow by the General. See that everything is ready.

18. The regiment goes by Taru, Nowshera, Akora, to Khyrabad. Supplies must be ready at every stage.

19. Have all tents quickly repaired. The bunniahs must lay in food of all sorts. Ten seers of milk are wanted at each stage.

20. The force has crossed the river. It has taken seven days' cooked food. The heat is great, and there is little water in the country.

April 1893.

1. The new settlement is to begin in Peshawar. Yes, I hear so. What is the first thing to do?

2. All the village lands must be carefully surveyed. Every field, ravine, hillock and boundary noted. The village accountant should be a good man.

3. How is the revenue calculated and fixed? At one rate on irrigated and another on unirrigated lands. Those fields at the head of the cut are charged most.

4. How is the boundary fixed towards the Independent border? There has been no regular arrangement. All this has led to incessant quarrels for over twenty years. Something must be done now.

5. Yesterday I went out shooting. I got to the river but could find no ford. Luckily there was a boat with one oar and a broken rudder. I got in and floated down stream.

6. A duck rose up on the right bank, which I shot. I missed two snipe on the left bank. A flock of geese were too far away. Owing to bad luck I secured merely four birds.

7. Why is sport so bad this year? The rain was little, and now all the jheels are dry, and the birds are leaving for Russian territory. They have a long journey before them.

8. The fields are now full of barley and wheat; the sugar-cane has all been cut. The quail are coming in. Send out the call-birds. You should

get sixty birds in the fields. In the autumn they are found in the cotton.

9. There was a hue and cry in the village. All was still. It came from the western quarter. The chowkidar ran along the lane and said a burglary had been committed in Hoti. The Khan was roused and fired his pistol at them.

10. Has the regiment finished its annual musketry? No, two days remain when the General will inspect them. Tell the lads to shoot well; the credit of the corps depends on them. Well done, lads, the regiment will head the list! You shall have your two months' furlough after the parade.

October 1893.

1. I am going out shooting to-morrow. Tell the shikari to be present at Nissatta, with six coolies, at 7 o'clock in the morning. Is there a ford there or ferry? What sport may I expect? At this season duck and geese are plentiful in the river, and snipe are to be had in the jheel close by. You may find some bustard too in the mustard fields.

2. Where is the lambardar? Why is he not here? Sahib, a burglary was committed last night in the village and he is sitting with the Thanadar, but he has sent his elder son. Tell me what happened. Thieves broke into the bunniah's shop which is near the mosque. It was midnight. A hue and cry party turned out, and one of the thieves was caught on the spot. It being a moonlight night, three of his companions were also identified.

3. Who is the arrested man? What is his profession? How many times has he been in jail? It appears he was a noted thief and outlaw. The village is of very bad repute, and its headmen are useless. How many times have the ricks been burnt? There is evidently enmity at the bottom of this, and the village must be fined.

4. The regiment will march next month for Rawal Pindi. How many men are on leave? How long has Jan Mahommed been absent without leave? To-day is the fifth day. It is said that he is suspected of murder in his village and therefore cannot return.

5. There has been a great deal of cholera this year. The men should be warned to drink river water, which is clearer than that in the wells. Be careful too that the supplies at each stage are fresh. At Akora the men must be careful of their rifles, as several thefts have occurred there.

6. What is the revenue of this village? Is the land irrigated or not? Much of the laud is rice land. Since the Swat canal was opened both rice and sugar-cane have been cultivated to a great extent. but the country is much more unhealthy than it was formerly.

7. Are there no hospitals? Yes, there are two, and the doctor sahib is very kind to the patients, who receive food and clothing free from Government.

8. What fresh news is there to-day from Swat? It is said that, owing to faction feeling and fighting among themselves, the country is being ruined. Travellers do not go that way now, all the roads being unsafe.

9. I hear a great deal of salt goes from Kabul to Peshbolak in the Jelalabad district. Are there no salt mines in Kabul? How is the salt carried? Chiefly by Powindahs on camels, but donkeys and mules are also used in great number by the Khattak carriers.

10. Select two sharp men from your regiment to visit the Kagan valley. They must report carefully on the state of the road and especially on the number of villages and the supplies which can be obtained from them. How far is Chillas from Balakot? How many fighting men can the neighbouring tribes turn out?

April 1894.

1. What day of the month is it? It is the sixteenth. Very well, I shall go out shooting on the twentieth. Tell my bearer to wake me at seven exactly, if I am still asleep then; and tell the shikari I shall want two fowls, twelve eggs, half a seer of ghee, some butter and ten and a half seers of atta on my arrival at Baboozai.

2. Last time I shot at Baboozai, I shot a markhor, three black partridge, a hare, four chikor, and would perhaps have shot some duck but my cartridges were beginning to get wet and would not go off.

3. Are you keeping the fast or not? All true Mahommedans should keep the fast and pray five times a day. Come with me if you can. Is the border quite quiet? Last year and the year before several raids took place in the autumn and winter.

4. When going to Mardan you cross the Kalpani stream. Be careful you cross by the ford; in other places the water in very deep. It is cloudy and cold to-day, and snow will probably fall in the hills. The steep cliff north of the village is in Independent Territory; so do not go there without an escort from the village.

5. My uncle's house was broken into last night, and some cash and jewels were stolen. A thief was arrested on the spot. Bring him before me. I do not believe your evidence. The complainant has blamed you. Sahib, he accuses me falsely, owing to an old enmity.

6. The regiment will march at 9 to-night. There will be a night attack on Sapri. Take some spare mules for the ammunition, as the road is very

difficult. There is no smoke, nor are the dogs barking, so I expect the village has been abandoned by the tribesmen.

7. There is a great deal of sickness this year, and cholera will most likely spread to Peshawar. Be careful the lines are kept quite clean, and give orders that no unripe peaches, water-melons or other fruits are allowed to be sold to the sepoys.

8. A chestnut mare was stolen last night from the Cantonments. Kuki Khel thieves are suspected. If trace of the stolen property can be found the tribe will be heavily fined.

October 1894.

1. Have you ever filed a suit against anyone? How do you act? I go to the petition writer; he brings out some stamped paper and writes my name on it; I then pay him, and give the petition into the court which has power to hear my case.

2. The reader of the court examines my paper; I then pay for the process fees. Defendant is sent for on a day fixed. We both appear with our witnesses; the case is heard and decided. Sometimes these suits last for years.

3. What troops are there in this station? Two regiments of European cavalry and two companies of sappers and miners. There will be a grand parade to-morrow. The General will inspect them.

4. Why is the General so particular about these parades? We are near the frontier and must always be ready for a fight. The men are daily at musketry. The men are repeatedly told that they must hit the thing fired at. If the soldiers cannot shoot well, they are no good.

5. Who is that man coming along running? He is the chowkidar of the village. What is he coming here for? Some affair must have taken place in his village and he has come to report it. This is the police station. Come and hear what he says. The man on that chair is the deputy inspector.

6. Well, Ahmed Khan, what is it? Last night at 11 P.M. I was going my rounds. It was dark, as clouds were overhead and rain was falling. I heard a cry in the eastern quarter of the village. I ran there and learnt this account. Jamal Khan was sleeping on his cot and was stabbed with a dagger in the stomach. Please come quickly.

7. What are these men doing? They are looking at the lands of the village of Jamal Garhi. With what object? Because the settlement is about to commence. The revenue on it is very light.

8. Can you tell me in what way this is done? The settlement officer first of all finds out everything regarding the village lands: these may consist

of hills and land that can never be cultivated; some depend entirely on rain and a few are irrigated fields. He fixes a separate rate on each. The revenue is collected half-yearly by the headmen and paid into the Tahsil.

9. Is there much sport in this country? Yes, there are chikor, seesi, duck and coolan. In the forest there are foxes, jackal, hares, deer. These last are very hard to find; shikaris have driven them away.

10. How do you arrange for quails? I ask a certain Khan to assist me. He sends men with call-birds to the cotton and wheat fields; these call and the quails come towards them. I go there with my gun before the sun is up and in this way can shoot forty or fifty birds.

April 1895.

1. Who are you? I am the son of a headman of a village. My name is Ahmed Khan and my father's Fateh Jang. We live in the village of Jamal Garhi. We hold fifty jaribs of irrigated and eighty-five of land which depends upon rain for its crops. Does this give you enough to live upon?

2. No, because the irrigated lands produce about five hundred rupees a year and unirrigated some two hundred rupees. Ours is a large family and we require about a hundred rupees every month. We have therefore to take to service.

3. My father has a pension of five rupees a month. My eldest brother is a jemadar in a cavalry regiment; my second brother is a havildar in the 1st P.I.; the third is a naik in the Border Militia. I am a deputy inspector in the Peshawar Police. I am in charge of Rustam thana. It is twenty miles from Mardan.

4. How is the village watchman appointed? He is selected by the headmen. He is then sent to the police for approval. His pay comes from the village. The pay is very small. The villagers look upon him as a spy of the police and put no trust in him. On this account his reports are usually false.

5. Why is that man running? He is coming to report some case. What is the matter, Akram? Last night I was going my rounds at 10 o'clock. I had got to the south of Mahàbat Khan's musjid when an alarm was raised in the eastern quarter.

6. I went and learned that the Khan had been stabbed. Who did this? It is difficult to say. There is great enmity in the place. This settlement has caused bitter feuds in the families. One cousin is hostile to the other cousin.

7. What orders have been received regarding the regiment? It will march at 5 A.M. for Chamkanni and halt for half an hour on this bank of the Bara. They cross by fords and boats to the other bank.

8. Attack the village. The men should take water and cooked food with them. It is a long march there and back. How many carts, camels and mules will be wanted for the regiment? Ask for them to be here to-morrow. Examine the carts carefully. The road is bad and has not been repaired for years. Order wheat, barley, rice, Indian corn and grain to be collected at every stage. The bunniahs are very troublesome.

9. What game is there in this district? Quail come in during spring and autumn. Deer have all disappeared. Now and then you see a hare. I have only seen twenty in twenty-five years.

10. A report has come in that the Mehtar of Chitral has been killed. How did this happen? He was out hunting, when his stepbrother murdered him. Is there any reason for this? Yes, the last claimed the throne. The affairs in Chitral are in a disturbed state.

October 1895.

1. Who are those men? They are members of the settlement office. What is their business here? They are measuring the lands of the village of Landi. The new settlement has been started. The people are afraid that the revenue will be greatly increased.

2. This will be a great sorrow to the poor landowners. Last year their autumn crops were destroyed by locusts. These were rice, cotton, Indian corn and sugar-cane. This year the spring crops were burnt up. They consist of barley and wheat. A new canal is being made. If this turns out a success the landowners will be pleased.

3. What are you going to do now? I am going to the petition writer. I will purchase some stamped paper from him. He will then write out my claim against Saadat Khan. I will then produce it before the civil judge and ask him to fix a day for the hearing of my claim.

4. Settle the claim by arbitration. Friends of both parties can do this easily. If you go into the court the matter will never end. You will be ruined by the pleaders. Remember what a Sikh said about the courts in the Punjab. Do not go near them.

5. What building is that? It is the police post of Khazana: three miles farther on is the Daudzai Tahsil. A large crowd is collected by the gateway. Let us go and see what is the matter. That man with the grey beard is the deputy inspector. He is a capital hand at taking bribes. Keep silent and let me do the talking.

6. Peace be on you, Khan! I hope you are well. What is this crowd collected here for? Fateh Khan lambardar is a man of seventy years of age. He married a pretty girl of fourteen. Her parents forced her to do so. She

is in love with Ahmed Khan. Last night, as the old man slept, the young man entered the courtyard. The chowkidar of the house fired at and killed Ahmed Khan.

7. The regiment will parade at 5 A.M. on Friday. Why has this order been issued? Because the regiment has been ordered on service. Three brigades are to assemble at Dargai on the 1st April. They will ascend the Malakand Pass and descend into Swat. The object of this advance is to punish Umra Khan, who has invaded Chitral contrary to orders.

8. Have you arranged for the carriage? Five thousand camels and fifteen thousand donkeys have been collected. Three parts at Nowshera and the fourth part at Mardan. What have you done about supplies? At each stage a bazaar has been formed. Food of every description for men and cattle has been stored up.

9. I want to have a day's shooting. How am I to get it, and where? Get up at 5 A.M. to-morrow. Walk down to the river. It has no ford, but you can get across in a boat. The jheel lies about half a mile from the ferry. You can get snipe, duck and goose. Will this be sufficient for you?

10. Here is another plan. Send for call-birds to the cotton fields near Regi. You might get fifty quail in a morning. Then walk over the plain for hare, sand grouse and bustard. At the skirt of the hills you will see partridge, chikor and seesi. The deer, urial and markhor have all disappeared from the country. I wish you every success.

April 1896.

1. I desire to bring in a civil suit. How can this be managed? Go to the petition writer and buy a piece of stamped paper. Write your petition on it and then hand it in to the court. The judge will read it and see what he can do.

2. The judge had the petition read to him. He wished to summon the defendants for the 5th of April. The plaintiff said this day was the Id-i-Ramzan and another day should be fixed. The judge said, "Your opinion is quite correct."

3. A new settlement is being carried out. What sort of lands have you in this village? Are the lands irrigated from wells or from the rivers? What is the water tax? Who fixed it? To whom does the appeal go? I hope it will be rejected.

4. There is no hope for an appeal. The tahsildar is a bad lot. The Qanungo does not know his duties, and the Patwari is equally bad. Our hope lies in the Settlement Officer. They say he is a very able man and exceedingly impartial.

5. What is your name, Khan? What village do you belong to? I come from Khazana. It lies beyond Daudzai. You must come over a bridge of boats. There is no ford to help you. What a misfortune all this is!

6. The produce of the village is this: wheat, barley, millet, in the spring. Then there is fruit and vegetables of sorts. Later on we have melons, grapes, etc. Last of all, Indian corn and sugar-cane. Cotton also grows well.

7. Last night there was a disturbance in the village. The noise was in the eastern quarter; a shot was fired. The chowkidar ran to see what was the matter. A man jumped down into the street, from thence he ran into the mosque and said he was a seeker after knowledge.

8. The thanadar received the news. He considered the matter well. He said, this is a made-up case. If I say any more it may end in my ruin. God help the poor man who is in this calamity!

9. The regiment will march to-morrow for Jamrud. See that all supplies are ready. The bunniahs must have everything collected. Their carriage must also be at hand. What carriage do you require?

10. Carts from here to Jamrud. How many? About two hundred. Then how many camels? About five hundred. What weight can they carry? About five maunds for each camel. I trust this may be all correct.

October 1896.

1. Who is that? Which do you want? I see many people going along the road. That fat man seated in the ekka with a long grey beard. His name is Zaman Khan, and he is held in great respect by the people. He has been twice to Mecca.

2. Has he any other good qualities? Yes; first he is liberal to the priests, to seekers after knowledge, and beggars. He is famous for his hospitality. His guest-house is always full. May the Almighty protect him always! So be it!

3. Akbar, where are you going? I have a civil suit against Ibrahim. He owes me 165 rupees. I want to see the petition writer. When the petition is ready and process fee purchased, I will go to the judge. If Ibrahim's property is not attached he will escape across the border.

4. What is a settlement, and what does it mean? The measurement of land, the fixing of rates and the very utmost revenue. The landowners are in great affliction. This calamity comes after every twenty years. There are separate rates on *maira*, well and irrigated lands.

5. That is the village chowkidar. He is going to the police station. What has occurred? He was going his rounds last night. It was about 10 P.M. and everything was still. As he reached the musjid a disturbance

arose in the eastern quarter. He ran to see what had occurred. The head-man, Ashraf, had been shot in the courtyard.

6. The police inspector went to enquire. He asked Ashraf who had wounded him. "Whom do you suspect?" "I was asleep on my cot; a man jumped into my courtyard and the noise roused me. I stood up. The thief fired his pistol at me. My cousin, Qadir Khan, is my sole enemy. He is also my heir. If I die, everything goes to him. Arrest him quickly."

7. What is the number of your regiment? What is your colonel's name? Tell me something about it. Our station was Jhelum. Orders came in April to proceed to Chitral. We came by rail to Nowshera. We got down there. Tents, mules, camels, carts had been prepared and were ready. We encamped by the Kabul river.

8. Supplies of rice, wheat, barley, dhall, (clarified) butter, grass, chopped straw and wood were all ready. The Kabul river was in flood. The bridge of boats was gone. The regiment crossed in boats. It was difficult work, and took six hours. Mardan was reached at sunset. We halted there two days.

9. What sport is there now? Quail are just in. Shall you want call-birds? Yes, send me two to the cotton fields. So-and-so got fifty quail yesterday. Go very early. After sunrise they fly away far. Shoot straight and don't miss.

10. Snipe can be found in the jheel; duck, goose, coolan by the banks of the river; partridge, black partridge, hare, deer in the jungle and high grass; seesi, chikor in stony ravines; whilst urial and markhor can only be discovered with great trouble on the difficult cliffs.

April 1897.

1. Where are you going to, Aslam? To the *kacheri*. What is your business there? I wish to see the petition writer. Akbar owes me three hundred rupees. My claim has extended over three years, and he has not up to date paid me a single pice.

2. What can the petition writer do for you? I will buy stamped paper from him. He will then write out my claim and I will give him the process fees. My papers will then go before the judge. He will read my complaint and summon the defendant to appear before him by a certain date.

3. What is a settlement? What benefit does it confer on the people? It fixes all rights and the share of revenue paid to Government. Is it always the same? Not so.

4. There is one rate on well lands; another on lands that are flooded, a separate one on *maira* crops. Then sugar-cane gives a larger profit than mustard. Cotton is also taxed less. A separate charge falls on each produce.

5. Who are you, Khan? I am the headman of Khazana. What is your business now? I am going to the police station. My house was broken into last night. The thieves took away two thousand rupees. Do you expect to recover anything?

6. The Thanadar is not loved by the people. They say he is a friend of thieves and bad characters. He shuts his eyes to their bad deeds. They give him a share of the plunder. It is no wonder then that crime increases daily in the district.

7. What game is procurable now? Do you want partridge or chikor? Snipe have come in. Duck are abundant on the Kabul river. Geese can be found near Pabbi. Fish either at Abazai or Nausatta.

8. Tell the shikari to take you to Mathra. You will find quail there. Hare in the open plain. Sand grouse near the water. Bustard close to the hills. Markhor just below Lakka Sar. Shoot straight and do not miss.

9. Your regiment is ordered to Malakand. It will march on Saturday. The General inspects it on Friday. Be very careful that everything is ready. What transport do you require? One hundred carts, five hundred mules, six hundred camels.

10. Tell your bunniahs to have all supplies ready at Taru, Nowshera and other stages. It is the winter season, so lots of wood will be wanted.

October 1897.

1. Who are you? What is the name of your village? How far is it from here?

2. You say that your village is 10½ kos from here to the north. Which road goes to it, the right or left hand one?

3. The road is straight. It climbs the ridge; there are stones and big trees. You will find an ambush of Mohmands, 394 men; the night will be dark.

4. How can we escape them? Can we go through the fields? No, there is a steep cliff in front of you. 2¾ kos in front you will find ravines.

5. Praise God! we have escaped. Only seven men were wounded, and no one was killed. They are not good shots but fine swordsmen.

6. The headmen will have to give hostages, and the tribal allowances will be stopped. Tell him to cut all the maize crops. Place sentries over the threshing floors. Break the ploughs and shoot the bullocks.

7. I brought my pistol and wore a grey sheet over my body. My feet were bare; I left my sandals at home. I was so near that if he had fired at me he would have hit me; but he fired at the guide and missed.

8. The village has two quarters, the upper and the lower ones. My grandfather is the senior headman. He is a greybeard.

9. He came at noon one day last year in the spring across the border. He is coming again this year in autumn. His betrothed is there.

10. There is a raid on Sherpur. They hid arms in the crops. An old woman saw them and raised the alarm. The hue and cry went out. I was wrongly seized.

April 1898.

1. Oh, Pathan! May you not be tired! What village is this? May you not become poor! It is Spinkamr.

2. Whose son are you? Who was your grandfather? Are you married? How many sons have you? I am the son of the head lambardar. Zabta Khan, who was killed in the fight with the Buners, was my grandfather. He was a celebrated man. I have married two wives and have three sons. The eldest is 7½ years old, the youngest is in arms.

3. Are your lands good? Have you a good harvest this year? Our fields are mostly unirrigated. The locusts have done much harm. They constantly come and eat the corn.

4. To whom do these hills belong? Do your cattle graze there? The hills are within the borders of the Adam Khel country and do not belong to us. The Adam Khel make us pay one young goat yearly. They oppress us much.

5. Where is the road to Michni? Do you see that gap in the hills and that white stone? The road passes to the left of it under the black cliff. Horse and foot can go along it.

6. Stand! Post the sentries on all the hillocks round the camp. Make walls to the north and west. The tents are white and can be seen from afar on a clear night. Put grey sheets over them. To-night there will be a moon, and the enemy will shoot.

7. How many hostages will you give us—sons of old men of influence? If you do not, the tribal allowance will be stopped.

8. The river is strong, but we must cross it. There is a ford, but it is dangerous, and many men may be lost if a flood comes. Get inflated skins, tie them together with ropes and place them under the bank.

9. How many horses, camels, donkeys and sheep are collected? Chaff, gram and every kind of fodder will be wanted for them.

10. This is my betrothed. She was given me by her uncle. The wedding feast did not take place at the proper time, as she was enticed away by her lover. This will give rise to a blood-feud, for I am ashamed.

11. The dogs are barking. See if there is a thief. If not, throw a stone at them. Look! you missed the dog and hit the hen. She will not lay any more eggs, for her leg is broken.

12. It is raining heavily. Yesterday there was a strong wind. It is probable that snow will fall on the high hills.

October 1898.

1. Where do you live? Is it far from here? Yes, I live at Nurpur, 15 kos from here.

2. On what business have you come? Have you got any companion? What is your tribe? I suspect that you are a rifle thief, you look like an Afridi.

3. No, I am a poor man. I have come to the city to buy bullocks. My own bullocks have died. I shall buy that white one and this black one. They are fat.

4. Is there any shooting in this country? Yes, there are lots of duck and snipe. If you go to the jheel on the left-hand side of the road to Mooltan you will find game.

5. On the top of that hillock there is a large fort. On the further side there is a village. It has four quarters. Sarfaraz is the headman of the southern quarter. He is a young man. He will be a tyrant when he is old.

6. Why are the men running? There has been a raid. The Afridis have driven off 225 head of cattle. They wounded five men with swords. One may die. The watchman has put him on a bed and has taken him to the hospital. His arm is cut off and his shoulder is wounded.

7. The road has many trees on each side. It is a straight one. Where does it go to? It crosses the river at Sherpur by a boatbridge. On the further bank there is a sandy plain. You can only go there slowly.

8. Very well, lead my mare after me. I will walk. Tell the syce to put the blanket on, for it will rain. Wind your turban round my gun. It will get wet.

9. There are very many bushes and stones at that spot. There is a ravine there. In it there are fields. Last year wheat, barley, maize, cotton, and rice were cultivated there. There is a water-course there. The fields are irrigated at night by small channels.

10. See that there is fodder for all the horses and mules. Post sentries all round the camp. See that their rifles are loaded. We shall all be ashamed if any guns or property is stolen.

April 1899.

1. What is your name? Where do you live? I live in Bazar. What is your tribe? I am a Khusrogi. Your people are great robbers. Sahib, we have neither lands nor cattle, and if we do not rob we must starve.

2. How far is it to the top of the Pass? It is 2½ kos. Is the road steep? Yes, but laden mules can pass over it. When you get to the top can you see Tangi? No, it is hidden.

3. What village is that? That is Booria. What crops are grown by the villagers? Sugar-cane, wheat and Indian corn. Is the land all irrigated? No, some land depends on rain. Why do you not grow rice? The water-tax is excessive.

4. Is there any shikar in the neighbourhood? Yes, in those rice fields you will find some snipe and duck. In the desert you will come across oubara and sand grouse.

5. Who is that man? That is the deputy inspector of police. What is he doing here? Sahib, there was a murder in the village last night. Was there a moon? No, it was dark. Where was the crime committed? In the southern quarter of the village. Why have the police arrested all these old men? It is useful to annoy rich peeple.

6. The regiment marches at daybreak to-morrow. Is there a bridge at Abazai, or have we to cross in a boat? There is a boat which is worked on a rope. Tell the rearguard they must have food for the day with them. The colonel's horse stumbled this morning, but the sahib was not hurt.

7. It is reported that a raiding party is hidden in the hills close by. They are about 50 strong. How are they armed? A few have Martinis and Sniders, but the rest have only muzzle-loaders and matchlocks. Tell the Subadar that the sentries must be doubied to-night. Make a hedge of thorns near the guard. After dark no fires may be lighted.

October 1899.

1. How far is it to the camping-ground? It is about 2 hours' march. Is there plenty of water? There is a good spring about 200 paces to the east, above the water-mills.

2. What supplies are obtainable? There is a Ghilzai camp about ½ a kos to the north, and the Ghilzais can supply wood, grass, sheep, milk, fowls and eggs.

3. The patrol will go up the valley as far as the top of the pass. Dc not cross the watershed, as that is our boundary and beyond it is Independent Territory. Tell the daffadar to be back by sunset.

4. What is that firing? It is only the young men of the village firing at marks. Some of them are very good shots.

5. Sahib, I want a week's leave without pay. My grandfather died yesterday evening and I am his heir. If I do not go home my cousins will seize the inheritance.

6. Why is this land not cultivated? Sahib, the land over the water channel is barren, because we cannot get water on to it, and owing to the drought the land below the channel has not been cultivated this year, as there has been so little water in the river.

7. It is thundering and the sky is very cloudy. I think we shall have a storm to-night. It is snowing now on the tops of the hills.

8. We always send cattle escorts when we send our cattle to graze. The people of the hills are great thieves; besides, the leopards and wolves are very bold and carry off our goats.

9. Why are you throwing stones at him? Sahib, he abused and struck me. He is my brother-in-law, and we quarrel whenever we meet. I did not strike him.

10. One man and one old woman have been killed and two little children seriously wounded. The people of the village will have to pay the blood-money and wound-money and a fine of Rs. 1,000. The Maliks will be held responsible for the payment of the whole amount within one month.

11. A raid took place on Thursday. Two buffaloes and forty cows were carried off. The raiders, who are said to be Gumatti outlaws, went off in the direction of the Waziri border. A pursuit party from Kanda village went after the raiders, but were unable to recover the cattle, being only armed with flint-lock guns, while the raiders had Martinis and Sniders.

12. Did not the villages warn the Border Police Post? They beat a drum, but did not send a man to the post, and the men there did not hear the noise of the drum because of the wind. The cavalry patrol saw the raiders from a distance, but could not attack them, as the paths were very bad and their horses could only go very slowly.

April 1900.

1. What is the date? It is Friday the 29th. Remember that we start the day after to-morrow. Send the camels with the tents on with the advance guard, and we will ride out the first march, starting about midday. I will ride the grey mare and you can take the bay. We will take the greyhounds with us, as we may possibly see a hare or two on the plain.

2. Had you told me earlier I would have come yesterday. I could not help it. I sent a man to you three days ago, but he lost his way. He says that he met a party of raiders and hid in a cave all night to escape them, but this may be merely an excuse.

3. While the regiment were encamped at Pabbi on the night of Thursday 2nd inst. some rifle thieves cut a hole in the guard tent and stole two Lee-Metford rifles and one bolt. The sentries outside the camp fired at the thieves

as they were running away and, it is believed, hit one, as bloodstains were found in the nullah this morning.

On the same night two boxes of Martini-Henry ammunition, one of blank and one of empty cases, were stolen from the railway station at Nowshera. It is said that the rifles and ammunition were smuggled across the frontier hidden in coffins.

4. A raiding party of about seventy Aka Khels raided the mills of the village of Landai a fortnight ago. They carried off about twenty loads of flour and wheat, which they loaded on donkeys. There were tracks of flour all the way to the border.

5. The regiment will parade to-morrow at daybreak for a reconnaissance towards Shabkadr. Supplies for two days will be taken on regimental transport. No tents will be taken. No wheeled transport can be taken, as the unmetalled roads are very heavy owing to the recent rain.

6. How do you divide your tribal subsidy? There are eleven elders in my section, and the subsidy is divided among them in proportion to the number of fighting men of each family. My own share is Rs. 91 a year. I divide this among my own relations, giving one-fourth to be divided among those of my cousins and nephews with whom I am on good terms.

7. The usual way of settling small disputes in Tirah is to refer the case to some Mulla, who is supposed to give his decision according to Muhammedan law, but in most cases the Mulla is bribed.

October 1900.

1. Where did you buy that Lee-Metford rifle, and how much did you pay for it? I bought it in Mardan for Rs. 1,900, Kabuli; it is one of the rifles taken during the expedition. Stolen rifles can sometimes be bought in Jam and these are cheaper, as there is a risk of having to give them up.

2. Is there any shooting in this part of the country? Very little indeed, sir. The country is so barren that there is nothing for the birds to eat. There used to be chikor in the ravines and hills, but the village boys used to catch them with snares, and there are now none left. The ravine deer, too, have all been shot.

3. Owing to regiments containing Afridis having been ordered to China, numbers of men on leave in Tirah have been suddenly recalled. The men are very keen on going to China, as many of the older men of the tribe, who were in the last China war, have told them tales of the wealth and fertility of the country.

4. It is reported that the cholera in Kabul is spreading rapidly in the country round, and that hundreds of deaths are occurring daily in the city

itself. The Amir has ordered gunpowder to be burnt in the streets, and the people are giving large sums in alms.

5. This year three tigers were sent up to Kabul as an offering to the Amir. They were in a cage which was on a bullock cart. In the pass a wheel came off the cart, and the cage was damaged. We had to put a guard over the cart for the night and in the morning sent down a carpenter to repair it.

6. A man came running towards us. He said he was a Khusrogi, and that he had seen a raiding party of seventeen well-armed men on the southern slope of the Bori Pass.

7. Do you know who threw the stone which hit you? Yes, a boy from Ahmed Khan's village hit me with a stone, but he says that he did not hit me on purpose and that it was an accident. If he will take his oath to this I will be satisfied.

8. The Bangashis and Khattaks of the Kohat District are fond of dancing and singing, but the Afridis consider this undignified, though the wealthier men among them often hire professional musicians to sing and dance for their amusement.

9. The river has been very full all this summer and the water has been so muddy that there has been very little fishing. When the water clears the fishermen from Lalpura will come down with their nets.

10. The men of the Katta Kushta outpost saw a herd of markhor on the hills to the north of the tower last Thursday. The jemadar took a sepoy's Snider rifle and went after the herd. He shot a fine markhor with horns about five span long.

11. How did that felt get wet? Put it in the sun to dry. Has the blacksmith come? No, he has not come yet. He ought to be here by now, as I got a message yesterday from Jan Khan that he would be here early this morning.

12. Why have the crops in this field failed while those in the other fields are so good? Sir, my neighbour who owns the land above mine is my enemy, and cut the water off when my crops were beginning to ripen.

13. This is a bad year for poor people. Owing to the want of rain in the Punjab all kinds of grain have become very dear. We now can only eat bread made of maize and millet.

14. Have the Aka Khel committed any raids lately? Since the people of Phandu killed three of the raiders last winter with spades they have not dared to raid openly, but they commit thefts in the neighbourhood of the villages.

15. How was Kuchai killed? Sir, yesterday evening our shepherds came

back with the flocks from the grazing grounds, and one of them reported that a cow buffalo which he had taken to graze in the morning was lost. The men of the village went out in every direction to search, and Kuchai met two thieves leading the buffalo away. He tried to stop them, and one of the thieves shot him dead with a revolver.

April 1901.

1. When the troops started for the manœuvres professional thieves followed them to get rifles. Officers commanding regiments and detachments were warned, and they made special arrangements. Informers supplied by the police were sent with the troops to point out any well-known bad characters.

2. A sentry was shot on Tuesday night by an outlaw. The murderer hid in a culvert and fired at the sentry as he was standing at ease. The bullet hit him in the hip, and he bled to death in a few hours.

3. The troops in camp protected themselves as if they were on active service. The camps were surrounded with breast-works and barbed wire, and the hills round were picketed as a protection against snipers.

4. What prices do you trans-border people pay for arms and ammunition nowadays? Sir, since the Tirah expedition prices have nearly doubled. Ammunition is especially hard to get, owing to the new regulations which have been introduced in regiments. If we can get caps, we reload our old cases six or eight times.

5. Who is this deaf and dumb boy? He is the grandson of one of the Kuki Khel elders. When he was an infant his nurse dropped him, and he has since been an idiot and subject to fits.

6. Here is a list of 11 bad characters living in your villages. You must give security for their good behaviour. For each I require a security of Rs. 350, and the sureties must be men of good position, who possess lands or houses to at least double that amount.

7. Who are you, where do you come from, and what are you doing here? I am an armourer by trade, and I live in the Kohat Pass. I have come in here to buy steel and other materials for my work. I was arrested by the Border Police on the road, but was released as there was nothing against me.

8. The Khattak carriers used to do a large trade in salt with Kabul. Do they still carry this on? No, since the Badakhshan salt-mines have been opened, the Amir discourages any import from India.

9. Select two sharp men from your company to visit the route through the Mohmand country. They must report carefully on the state of the road, especially where it crosses the ridges, and must note what parts of the road are not practicable for wheeled transport.

10. Shortly after entering the pass we saw numbers of vultures and hawks flying about. Guessing that there must be some dead animals to attract them, we searched in the ravine and soon found the body of a young boy who had evidently been murdered. The body was stripped naked and covered with dagger wounds. Further on we found a little girl slightly wounded hiding in some bushes. She said that her brother had loitered behind the caravan and had been set on by thieves. One of the thieves had thrown a stone at her which hit her on the right ear and knocked her down, and the others had seized her brother who resisted and was killed.

October 1901.

1. A column of cavalry with two guns started at dusk yesterday for Shabkadr, where a considerable force of Mohmands is reported to be threatening the fort. It is possible that small parties of tribesmen may attempt to break through our line of outposts, so all detachments should be warned to be on the alert.

2. Do you shoot ? No, I have not been able to afford a rifle or shot gun and have only a flintlock. I cannot shoot animals or birds flying or running, and they are so much shot at here that it is very difficult to find them asleep.

3. The snipe are beginning to come in; a considerable number flew over my village yesterday; they were flying high and probably settled in the artillery jheel.

4. As we approached the wall of the village a dog began to bark. We thought that the people would wake and that we should be discovered, but a boy who was sleeping in the guest-house got up and threw a stone at the dog and lay down again. No one else stirred.

5. The plaintiff stated that the defendant and his servants had repeatedly interfered with and damaged the water-cut which irrigates his fields. On the day in question a strong party of the defendant's men came to his village and began, as usual, to break down the bank of the channel.

6. Plaintiff collected all the men he could, but the defendant's party were too strong for him. They almost entirely destroyed his water channel, cut and destroyed two fields of standing corn, and burnt a mill after breaking the mill-stone.

7. The defence is that a party of defendant's men were passing plaintiff's village when they were suddenly attacked and abused by the people of plaintiff's village, several of them being struck with stones and considerably injured.

8. Although the crops, especially maize and millet, have been unusually good this year in Peshawar and the surrounding districts, prices still remain very high. The reason for this is that all surplus grain instead of being

sold cheap in Peshawar is sent by rail to those districts where scarcity still prevails.

9. Three columns will start from Peshawar and one from Nowshera on Friday evening, meeting at Pabbi at daybreak on Saturday. The Nowshera column will consist entirely of cavalry and mounted infantry. The three Peshawar columns will consist of a wing of British Infantry, one regiment Native Infantry, one squadron cavalry. Four field guns will go with No. 1 column, which will go by the main road. No. 3 column will go by Chamkanni and No. 2 column by Daudzai. No. 1 column will have cart transport and the others mules and camels. Three days' rations will be taken, and the troops will return to their stations on Monday evening.

April 1902.

1. What do you do with your rifles at night on service or on manœuvres? We used to stand them up round the tent pole and chain them together, but now each man digs a hole under his bedding, places his rifle in it and sleeps on the top of all. Since we have adopted this device we have not lost a single rifle.

2. Do you see that dark mound near this bank of the stream? Occupy that with your company and keep the enemy from using the crossing. Do not fire more than is absolutely necessary. Make your men keep under cover, and don't let them crowd together when they retire.

3. Sahib, I started from the fort, as ordered by you, at 4 A.M. with my patrol. We took the Karamma road and reached the pass without seeing anyone coming or going. We had scouts out on every side so that we might get timely warning of an ambush. On our way back two shots were fired from high up on the hill to our right. There was no sign of the bullets.

4. Sahib, I have a petition to make. What is it? The stock of my rifle is cracked and I want it bound with wire. Will you let your armourer do it for me? Yes, if you will pay him; but if the stock is cracked through, binding it will be no good.

5. Who are you? My name is Asaf, and I am a smith. I want to enlist. You know quite well that men of low caste, such as smiths, carpenters, bakers, musicians, etc., are never enlisted as soldiers. If you can play or learn any musical instrument you might be enlisted in the Band.

6. Why is that woman weeping? She says that she is weeping because her mother-in-law beat her. Ask her mother-in-law why she beat her, and tell her that it is not proper for her to beat her daughter-in-law in a public place like this.

7. There has been very little rain in Tirah and Afghanistan during the

past winter and spring, and there is great scarcity of water. The springs are very low and are not unlikely to fail altogether, and the unirrigated crops are withering. The Bara rice is the only crop which will not fail; this is well irrigated.

8. A woman, the wife of a weaver in Naisatta, was delivered of twins on the evening of Tuesday, 11th March. As soon as they were born they got up, walked across the room, seated themselves upon the doorstep of the hut and began to talk. The people of the house, who were terrified, heard them prophesy that there would be war and famine during the year. The children died the same night, and it is suspected they were smothered.

October 1902.

1. Take the recruits to the range to-morrow, and start at sunrise, so as to be there as early as possible. Take 10 rounds of ball and 10 rounds of blank for each man.

2. See that the swords of your troop are taken to the armourer to-day and properly ground. They should be sharpened thoroughly both at the edge and point.

3. The regiment has been ordered to Cherat and will march to-morrow at dawn. Which is the best road to take? We want, of course, to go the shortest possible way, but we have only wheeled transport, so we must choose a fairly good road.

4. What is this, and who is this boy whose face is smeared with blood? Call him here. Boy, what have you been doing, and who has beaten you? Sahib, I threw a stone at a dog, and Jan Khan came up and said it was his dog, and then he took a stick and beat me as you see.

5. A raid took place on Wednesday night. About 20 Aka Khels hid in the ravines of the Kajouri plain and came out at night and broke into the house of a grain-dealer in the village of Sheikhan.

6. The villagers resisted, and one man was killed and one wounded. As the raiders cannot be arrested because they live in Independent Territory, the tribe will have to be fined for the raid, and will have to pay blood-money for the man killed.

April 1903.

1. Sit down on the bed. Will you drink tea? Will you eat anything? It is very kind of you. Put very little milk in the tea. I will eat some eggs.

2. I was with my regiment at the taking of Delhi. Therefore I was summoned to the Durbar. Much honour was done to us who had served Government in the Mutiny.

3. I hit Sher Muhammed on the head with a spade. I then took refuge with a Waziri Malik. Life among the Waziris is very trying. If I come back, will the police arrest me? I am ready to pay compensation.

4. I missed the ford and had to swim for my life. My wet clothes were very heavy, but I reached the far bank. Next day I had fever. I have no money to buy quinine. Will you not give me some?

5. Our land is unirrigated. There has been no rain. The ground was too hard to plough, and we have no crops. We cannot pay our revenue.

6. Who is this tall man? He is my father's brother. I will have nothing to do with him. You are all well-known thieves. Cut off my beard, cut off my nose, if we were ever suspected of bad conduct.

7. The General will come on Monday. You must picket the hills on either side of the tonga road. Last year some scoundrel fired at him. We must take care that nothing of the kind occurs again.

October 1903.

1. Come in and sit down and tell me all your news. What are your rice and maize crops like this year? Is your mare in foal, and have you got a good price for your wheat? What has happened to the old man who killed Sarfaraz?

2. I told him that if he worried Adam he would find trouble himself. He said I was a liar and it didn't matter, and he was as good as Adam. If Adam had not wounded his camel he would not have set fire to the house.

3. A raiding party of ten men has just started for British territory. Every one of them has a breech-loading rifle. They have one Lee-Enfield, five Martinis, and three Sniders, while the tenth man has a sporting magazine rifle that he stole from an Englishman who was shooting in Chitral last summer.

4. If these villagers send out their cattle to graze without any guard and refuse to send out a pursuit party after them when they are stolen, the Government will certainly refuse them compensation.

5. A bad character took up his position on the top of a small hill and fired shots at the convoy as it was passing.

6. The havildar went home on six months' leave, but he spent the whole time in his tower as his two cousins said they would kill him unless he paid blood-money for their father, his uncle, whom he had stabbed to death the year before.

7. If the General pitches his camp on that spot, there is danger that the picket at the water supply will be attacked from that pass.

8. My brother's son has committed a serious crime. He ran away with

a woman from a Turi village and absolutely refused to pay the compensation money. Thereafter he became an outlaw and a dependent of the Afridis, and I believe he now makes his living as a hired assassin.

April 1904.

1. To what village and tribe do you belong? Do you live far from here? Where are you going? I am the son of a Malik, and we are going to a marriage procession. The crowd behind are the common people who always come to the marriage feasts of great men.

2. I met Sher Dil the day before yesterday. He told me his house had been broken into in his absence by Wazirs, and if he had been at home they would certainly have killed him.

3. I have been out shooting. I got six couple of snipe and a swan. I lost a mallard, as my dog got a thorn stuck in his foot, went lame, and would not work. A coolie who was going to look for it among the reeds sank in the mud up to his waist.

4. A rumour has come in that the Hassanzai are going to attack the fort. They have secured as allies six hundred Swatis armed with breech-loading rifles. A force will be sent to meet them as soon as transport can be arranged.

5. Has your blood-feud with the Ali Khel been settled yet? How did it begin? My grandfather abducted the daughter-in-law of a Malik and killed her husband, who came after her with a rescue party. We have now paid blood-money and given them a girl in exchange.

6. We have been to Peshawar to get work, as snow falls in our village in winter. Now we shall take our cattle to the summer pasture-ground. We have two hamlets there—one on the sunny and one on the shady side of the hill.

7. Which is the shortest way to the top of the ridge for mules? We tried to get up the dry water-course to the north, but were stopped by a precipice about a thousand feet high. Is it possible to get up by the eastern spur?

October 1904.

1. Why are the horses at this changing station never ready? I have passed through this place seven times in the last month and have always been delayed here.

2. Sir, the syce is a very worthless fellow. I told him yesterday that you were coming through to-day, but he never pays any heed to what I say.

3. I was trying to shoot chikor and walking over the hills near Gulistan.

When I had nearly climbed the top of the highest peak I met an old man, whom a little boy was leading by the hand. I said to him, "Well met, blind man." He replied, "Salaam, sahib, I know you are not a man of this country by your voice and your bad pronunciation of Pushtu." At this we both laughed and went our respective ways.

4. I want to go from here to Spinwam to-morrow. How far is it? Can I get water and grass or maize stalks for my horse anywhere on the way, as I want to rest for two or three hours during the heat of the day? Of course it is necessary that I should be accompanied by a tribal escort. Will you please make all necessary arrangements?

5. What do you mean by rebuilding your tower? I told you last year, after the expedition was over, that Government would get seriously annoyed if anyone built a tower in this tract of country. I am afraid you will have to come back with me to Jhal and remain there until your tower is knocked down again.

6. Confound you, why cannot you do what I tell you? You had plain orders to bring my trap to Nahakki and wait for me there. So why you drive on over this vile road to Shabkadr is known to God only. I suppose you think yourself wiser than I am.

7. Take ten men with you and make your way with all speed on to the hills over that neck over which our road passes. Halt there and keep your eyes open, and if you see any armed men let us know. But do not open fire unless you are fired at.

8. Will your dog bite me? Come here, good dog, good dog. The dog has bitten me! Get out, you beast!

April 1905.

1. Come here and talk to me. What is your name? My name is Dauran. I am a shikari. I am well acquainted with all the marshes about here. The General Sahib stayed here for two days. He shot 115 snipe, 9 ducks, and 7 pigeons. Are there any sand grouse here? Yes, certainly; at the foot of the hills there will be some.

2. Who are you? We three are reservists of the 30th Biluchis; those four are discharged sepoys of the 26th Punjab Infantry. What do you want? We want service in the Wana Militia. This man is lame; that man is blind; those two are old; I will enlist the three others.

3. I am going to shoot to-morrow at Pezu. A tribal escort is not necessary, but send three parties of one non-commissioned officer and six men each to picket the Pass. They must start at 5.30 A.M.

4. Why have you been absent from duty? I have a blood-feud with

Alim Khan. He is my cousin. I was besieged in my tower. Tell me all about it. Sahib, it was a very bitter feud, but, thanks be to God, I have killed Alim Khan and his three sons, and now there is peace.

5. Abdulla's grandson eloped with the Malik's wife. He won't settle the case by payment, and through fear of the Malik he has run away. He now lives in Independent Territory under the protection of Baz Gul.

6. My land is all irrigated, half of it from wells, half from canals. I pay Rs. 50 each harvest as water tax. Our crops are wheat, barley, maize, millet and sugar-cane.

7. Yar Baz and Gul Khan took the flocks to graze this morning. On the road they met a mad dog. The dog bit Yar Baz. Gul Khan shot the dog.

October 1905.

1. "Oh, sir, do you not see that large flock of teal swimming in the pond there?" "Yes, how am I to get within shot?" "You must creep through this field of standing rice, taking care not to show yourself. You will then from behind that tree on the edge of the village water channel be able to shoot one barrel at them as they sit and the second as they rise." "All right. You come with me." "Sahib, if you had not coughed you would have shot many more. But you are a good shot."

2. "A raiding party came down last night and attacked the Tiarza post. I have just heard of it by telegram. You must send ten sowars at once to watch the pass between those two hills. You must also take twenty-five men on foot and camp with them on the spur over the pass. Stay there two nights—till Friday—and patrol the country each day in strong parties. Can you manage all right for rations?" "Of course, Sahib. Shall I send men from the Yusafzai or the Afridi company?" "Send ten Yusafzais and fifteen Afridis; they are so good on the hillsides. Jemadar Alam Gul will be in command of the whole party."

3. "Sepoy Adam Khan, you are charged with having murdered Subadar Abdul Wahab on the 15th August last, by shooting him in the back while he was asleep on a charpoy. You have heard the evidence for the prosecution, which seems to the Court sufficient to justify a conviction unless you can rebut it. Do you plead Guilty or Not Guilty?" "Sahib, I did not kill the man, I swear to God. I did not wake up till I heard the shot. They give evidence against me out of enmity." "Do you wish to produce witnesses in your defence?" "Sahib, I do not understand your English law. What witnesses have I? I am a poor man, but 100 men of my village will take oath of innocence on my behalf."

4. I was sitting on the hill near Spin Sukha with two men of the

advance guard of the convoy. We were waiting for the camels of the convoy to come in sight. They were hidden from us by a bend in the road. Suddenly Sepoy Azmat saw the foremost camel and exclaimed, "There they are." At the same moment we heard two shots. I thought they were from a Martini-Henry rifle, but Azmat, who knew the country well, said, "No, the Sahib is with the rearguard, and he is shooting at game."

5. "How much land does this canal irrigate?" "Sahib, we are zamindars and know nothing of measurements. Certainly the canal gives us enough water, but the people in the lower village, who have a right to the surplus water, say that we take too much for our lands which are at the head of the canal. They are going to bring a case against us, which will cost both sides a lot of money, and we shall all be put on security to keep the peace." "What fools you Pathans are! If instead of litigating you would only combine and dig the canal a bit deeper there would be plenty of water for all."

April 1906.

1. The Kuki Khels sent their cattle out to graze without an escort. A raiding party of Zakha Khels which had been lying in ambush carried off all the cattle. A pursuit party of Kuki Khels turned out and succeeded in recovering 30 head at a loss of one man killed and one wounded. They are now suing the Zakha Khels for blood-money and for the value of the cattle not recovered.

2. Owing to the extension of canal irrigation in Peshawar, the value of land in certain tracts has risen from Rs. 50 to Rs. 200 per acre. Formerly, this land, having no means of irrigation except rainfall, was of comparatively little value. The owners who were formerly offering this land for sale at low prices are now engaged in trying to extend their property by pre-emption suits; and those who had already disposed of their land are gnashing their teeth.

3. The distance as the crow flies is 7 miles, but the winding of the road makes the distance actually traversed in climbing the pass 12 miles. The hills on either side, though steep, are, owing to their configuration, not difficult to picket.

4. Lalgul said that Gul had insulted him, and that had it not been for fear of the police he would certainly have killed Gul. Gul denied the provocation and said that Lalgul had without reason assaulted him when he was ploughing.

5. A Wali Khel woman left her husband and went to the Turi Khels who refused to return her. The Wali Khels claimed the return of the woman

and Rs. 100 as compensation, failing which they said they would take an army against the Turi Khels. The latter sent a Qazi with a Kuran to try to effect a settlement.

6. The tribe gave 10 hostages and deposited 15 rifles as security. Three of these were Lee-Metfords, 10 Martinis (of which 4 were Pass-made), and 2 Sniders. Thirteen of these have already been redeemed, but the 2 Sniders are so worn as to be practically smooth bores, and there is little prospect of their owners troubling about them.

October 1906.

1. Last night after dark 27 camels carrying grain for the troops in Jandola were brought into the fort. The camels belong to Pawindahs and can go no further. You must endeavour to find others in the neighbouring villages to take their place, as the grain is urgently required. Impress on the owners of the camels which you will collect that they will get hire at favourable rates. How many camels will suffice? How much will each carry?

2. A policeman's life is not a happy one. The pay is small, the work is hard, there is not the same prestige about the force as about the army, and the uniform is ugly. Especially in Peshawar, what with night patrols, the supervision of bad characters, sentry duty over the Sahibs' bungalows, and ambuscades for raiding gangs, a man has little time to eat or sleep, let alone to wash or to pray as he should do.

3. What is the history of the feud between your family and that of your cousins who live in Mian Kilay? When did it begin and for how many generations has it been going on? I do not know why it is that you Pathans, who have a code of custom which prescribes the payment of bride-price, compensation for moral and material damages on all occasions, wound-money and blood-money, should go on killing each other even after payment has been made in accordance with custom.

4. Take 10 men who are good runners and go as fast as you can to the place where the stream from Sangroba falls into the Kurram River. There hide yourselves on the right-hand side of the road and wait. If you are lucky the raiding gang will probably be returning that way this evening or to-night, and as the moon is nearly full you ought to be able to render a good account of them. Challenge first and then shoot.

April 1907.

1. This woman says that you have beaten her. What have you to say for yourself? Sir, she lies. If I had beaten her I would have killed her. The real facts are these:—I was sitting in the village cleaning my rifle. This

woman has a dog, a pestiferous animal: it came sniffing round me. I told it to go away, but it paid no attention, so I hit it on the head with my cleaning rod. The woman came out and abused me vilely, but I said nothing.

2. What can I do for you, my man? You want to be made a naik, a very laudable ambition. Sir, I wish to take my discharge. I am very happy serving here, but things are going badly in my home. My uncle has just died, my father is very old, and my only brother has committed a murder and become an outlaw.

3. There has been a settlement between the two tribes. Three Paria Khel were killed and 2 wounded and the Paria Khel claimed for blood and wound-money. On the other hand the Babi Khel demanded very heavy compensation for an alleged affront to tribal honour. Both tribes have agreed to build a fort and to maintain in it a garrison of 20 men, of whom 10 will be found by each tribe.

4. What is all the excitement? The lambardar after collecting the revenue has just skipped over the border to Afghanistan. It appears that his wife had got herself talked about with Tor Khan. Yesterday he found them together and killed them both.

5. Yesterday a raiding party came to our village. The cattle had gone out without an escort. The pursuit parties of the other villages refused to turn out. I fired ten shots and every one of them missed. The raiding party consisted of 10 men, and each man's share was 3 cows. The spies report that the thieves are willing to return the cows on receipt of a ransom of ten rupees each.

October 1907.

1. Is your wound well? It appears to me that there is some dead bone inside it. Don't be afraid. I am going to examine the wound. I will not hurt you much. There, it is done. This piece has come out of it. But there is still another bit. It is caught in the flesh, and I cannot extract it without cutting. All right, if you like I can leave it for the present, but I could take it out in a moment, and you would not even feel the pain. It is out. Now wash the blood from it and cover the wound.

2. Come by this path. The ascent is difficult on that side. In fact one cannot ascend by it. The reason of it is that the cliff on that side rises straight up to the sky, and there is no path. Even this road is not free from trouble, for there is the fear of snakes in the dense grass, and in many places the ground is so slippery that persons have fallen down. If one's foot were to slip he is lost, for the ground drops in a sheer precipice to a great abyss below.

3. A raiding party entered our village last night and killed a man and his wife and carried off clothes and jewelry worth about Rs. 850, and one of the raiders killed another raider by mistake in the darkness. The villagers have only themselves to thank for their loss, as they were warned that a raiding party was expected; yet the village gates were left open and every one was fast asleep, although the dogs barked lustily and the cocks crowed.

4. Alam Gul's house was broken into on the 21st of last month, and a she-goat and two ewes were stolen. A pursuit party of Border Police and of District Police turned out and caught sight of the four thieves at the foot of the hills. Three managed to escape from sight, but the fourth was surrounded, and after firing many shots at the pursuit party was himself shot. The deceased had with him a Pass-made Martini-Henry rifle, a long Afridi knife, three packets of ammunition and six loose rounds.

5. The wife of a barber in Khoedad Khel country lately went to a Mulla and said: "My husband has beaten me." The Mulla warned the husband, whereupon the barber beat his wife in the Mulla's presence. The Mulla flung a stone at the barber which hit him on the head and killed him. The woman was much pleased, but the Khoedad Khel fined the Mulla Rs. 250, and paid the money to the barber's son as blood-money.

6. During the last few days the people of Kurram have believed a rumour that Government is going to bring plague upon them by putting medicine in their water, and by killing the rats, whose death they consider to be the cause of plague. The origin of the rumour has been traced to nomadic Jajis, returning from down country who are spreading reports which the ignorant people at once believe.

April 1908.

1. Tell the gardener that while I am away he must level the grass and take out all the weeds. He must also arrange to have the two big mulberry trees cut down. The wood of one will be sold by auction, but the other must be kept for firewood. Let him take care that the falling trees do not injure the bungalow. If the auction had been held at the time of the expedition I should have got a good price. But now, wood is cheap again as the contractors are selling all the supplies which they had collected.

2. There are a lot of duck sitting in the reeds. I shall sit in hiding behind these juar stalks. You will pass through the gap in the wall and take your stand behind the hillock. Mind you stoop as you walk and do not show yourself, lest you should spoil our chances of sport. The boatmen will put up the birds by throwing stones and clods. Once I tried to walk in the jhil

myself, but I got stuck in the boggy ground. The left barrel of my gun got filled with mud and I lost 145 cartridges.

3. The old woman was weeping because she had lost her only cow, which she said a thief had taken. The Thanadar laughed at her and said that if she had taken more care she would not have suffered this loss. Whereupon the old woman abused him and spat at him. The Thanadar then got angry and exclaimed: "That is the way with you people. You are adepts at abuse. You do not understand how difficult it is to investigate crime, especially in this part of the country where people prefer lies to truth."

4. The old man said, "I wonder why Government takes so much trouble to have our children educated. A lot of money has been spent in building a school in my village, but we Pathans don't much care for books and pens. I was brought up with the idea that a man should learn to shoot straight and to ride well. My grandson dare not even drive a trap, the coward! We Pathans are getting soft. A new age has brought new customs, and it is time I died."

October 1908.

1. What is all the excitement? An outlaw has just surrendered who went off last year. He was unhappy in the hills, for every one likes his own country best. He came in with his head bare, with a rope round his neck, and with grass in his mouth, and fell at the Hakim's feet and said, "I am your cow." The villagers watched the proceedings with much amusement.

2. May I be your sacrifice. I am a sinner in the sight of Heaven, but this crime I have not committed. The real offender is my uncle's son, who was assisted by my nephew. The police have charged me because I refused to supply them with firewood free.

3. How are your crops, uncle? My wheat was good, but my maize is very middling. It suffered greatly from the hailstorm of last month when there was thunder and lightning all night. I am now on the road to the Tahsil to apply for an advance of money.

4. I have now heard all your petitions and shall proceed to give you answers to them. Your petition about pardoning the outlaw is unreasonable. If he cares to surrender himself he will receive a fair trial according to the custom of the country. If he does not choose to do so you can keep him if you like, but you will be responsible if he commits any crime in British territory.

5. The raid was made by the Himmat Khels, who had an unreasonable and entirely fanciful grievance. They first cut the telegraph wire and then lifted 300 sheep which were grazing without a proper escort. They killed one

shepherd and carried off two others. The pursuit party turned out but was too late to do anything. Subsequently the two shepherds were ransomed on payment of Rs. 500.

6. The local authorities awaited their opportunity. A month later the Himmat Khels brought down a large trading party consisting of men and women, cattle, donkeys and camels carrying a variety of things, mostly timber and matting. They were all seized in reprisal, and enough of the animals and goods were sold to pay the value of the stolen sheep, the blood-money for the murdered shepherd and the ransom money of the other two shepherds, as well as a substantial fine. The Himmat Khels offered to bring the sum in cash if their property was released, and offered to lodge as security four Martini-Henry rifles, two Snider rifles, and two Lee-Metford rifles.

April 1909.

1. What is your name and tribe? Is your tribe well armed? Sir, we have 4,000 fighting men in our tribe, and over 2,000 of these have either Martini-Henry or Snider rifles. We have only about twenty Lee-Metfords, but even the boys have muzzle-loading guns, and many Persian Gulf rifles are now being imported.

2. Our land is poor. Most of it is unirrigated, and the crops produced are bad in a dry year. Even on our irrigated land we cannot produce rice or sugar-cane, and our wheat, barley and maize is not sufficient for our wants. Many of our young men go down to British territory every winter in search of labour, and some are also in service. These generally enlist in the Cavalry.

3. The families of Sher Dil and Afzal Khan have been at feud over women-cases for about four generations. Many on each side have been killed and wounded, and a certain number are still lying in prison. Now the Deputy Commissioner has appointed a jirga to settle the dispute, and after calculating all the blood-money, wound-money, etc., mutually due, the jirga has decided that Sher Dil's faction is owed one girl in exchange and Afzal's faction is entitled to Rs. 560 in cash.

4. News has just come in by wire from Jamrud that a raiding party is lying hid somewhere in the ravines near Matanni. Get your Company ready as quickly as possible and go out and look for them. Take fifty rounds ball and ten buckshot per man and do not wait to put on uniform. I have asked the Tahsildar to send as many tum-tums as possible, but you must not wait for them as they may not be forthcoming, and if they are they will overtake you on the road.

5. Why do you want leave? It is not the leave season. Sir, my family is in great trouble owing to the machinations of our enemies in the village.

My minor brother has been falsely accused in a murder case by Atlas Khan, who will certainly bribe a jirga to find him guilty unless there is someone to guard his interests, and our father is an old greybeard and very decrepit.

6. The Mullagoris and the British village of Sper Sang are always at loggerheads over grazing rights. According to an old settlement, which both sides accepted at the time, Sper Sang may graze its cattle in part of the Mullagori hills but not in other parts, and may cut grass and wood for its own use but not for sale. Both sides are quarrelsome, however, and now and then the Mullagoris carry off the Sper Sang cattle and hold them up to ransom, and Sper Sang in retaliation arrest any Mullagoris they can find. Last year if the Border Military Police had not intervened there would have been bloodshed, as both sides were openly drawn up facing one another and ready for battle.

October 1909.

1. Well, Malik, I am very pleased to see you. Why have you not come to see me for so long? When you last came you said you would come again when the quails were in and arrange some shooting for me, but you seem to have forgotten all about it. No, sir, I did not forget, but my enemies lay in wait for me and shot me, and though I escaped with my life I was on my back with fever for over two months.

2. How are the crops in your village this year, old man? Sahib, in some places they are very good and the people are well fed and happy, but my crops and those of all my relations and some other unfortunates have been destroyed by hail, and though we have bribed the Patwari as much as we can afford he will not bring the Tahsildar to inspect them, so that we may obtain a remission of revenue. We shall be ruined.

3. The Jemadar got six months' leave and went to his home in Tirah. He found, however, that his own cousin had eloped with the girl who was betrothed to him, and that in consequence there was a blood-feud between the two families; the elders of the tribe tried to make a money settlement, but failed.

4. Is it true that this village was raided last night? Yes, sir, a raiding party of 40 men from Independent Territory entered the village at the time of evening prayers and went to the house of Tara Singh, which they looted, and carried off his young son. The village pursuit party was not collected in time to recapture the boy, and they really only made a pretence of following up the raiders in order to avoid the imposition of a fine on the village.

5. What transport is procurable here, and is fodder, and water, good and

plentiful? Mules and ponies can be got at a day's notice in large quantities, but camels are not available so rapidly. They have to be brought in from the Khattak country. The water of the river is quite good, and grass is plentiful when the rains are good.

April 1910.

1. A report has been received that a party of Shinwaris raided Daulatabad last night. The villagers offered no resistance to the raiders, and no pursuit party turned out. A Hindu cloth merchant was the chief sufferer. He was compelled by threats and blows to reveal the spot where he had buried his cash. His two little daughters were carried off. If the two girls had been Mohammedans the villagers would probably have made some effort to release them.

2. The Malik said: "It is a good thing for a trans-borderman to serve in the Army. He learns to shoot well, and the drill makes him robust. He sees the world and gains experience. Some sepoys once went as far as China and came back all right. I wish I had entered Government service when I was a youngster. The Mulla scared me by saying that he would not bury me with proper rites if I took pay from the unbeliever. Government pays well and regularly, and nowadays a soldier can soon save enough money to buy a rifle and a wife."

3. The Wazirs held a jirga and decided that it was high time to do something. One of the elders said: "War is not a bad thing. Some of us will be killed and a few houses and some crops will be burnt. But in the end our allowances will be increased, the sahibs will get honours and decorations, and everybody will be satisfied. It is no use sitting still. My advice is that the Mullas should proclaim a religious war and that we should start raiding in British territory."

4. It is difficult to irrigate the land near the mouth of the Pass. The water flows along a ravine and much of it is lost in the gravel. To improve the supply of water it is necessary to make three short tunnels through the cliff. These will be blasted out by gunpowder. The water channel must be paved with brick. In former times the Moghuls used to irrigate this land by water brought from the Kabul river. There is no trace of their canal now.

PASSAGES FOR WRITTEN TRANSLATION. SET AT VARIOUS TIMES.

April 1900.

Mahmud had noticed with satisfaction the blows dealt at the empire of the Safis. The defeat of Safi Kuli Khan had been followed by the loss of the dependencies of the empire in the Persian Gulf and by attacks on its southern coast. The empire seemed distressed on every side.

Mahmud resolved to seize the opportunity. But just at this period he heard of the march on Farrah by the Abdalis to which I have referred. Farrah was garrisoned by the Persians. But at the moment the Persians were not to be dreaded. But the case would be different were that place, then a place of strength, occupied by men who, though Afghans, were Abdalis. Before dealing his blow at Persia, he resolved then to march to the relief of Farrah. There he met Azadulla, killed him and defeated his army. From Farrah he took a south-westerly route across the Seistan Desert and then moved towards Kirman. Surmounting great difficulties he reached Kirman and caused his authority to be acknowledged in the Province of which that town was the capital.

October 1900.

It is said that the name of Lukman for the following reason became famous as Khattak.

Lukman, Utman, Usman and Jadran, all four went out hunting. Three or four girls, also of Afghan birth, had gone out to the plain, so they met one another. The former said, "Come, let us four cast lots for these four girls: this is excellent sport." Lukman was the eldest of them and would not consent to casting lots, and said, "I will first select the one I prefer, and do you cast lots for the other three." They accordingly did so. Lukman selected the one of the four who was arrayed in the finest apparel, but when he looked at her, her beauty was not equal to her clothes.

The rest were superior to her in good looks, so the other brothers cast lots for them and took them according to the lots. Directly they knew of Lukman's adventure, they said with shouts of laughter: "Lukman has got into the mire." There is a saying among the Pathans, if anyone by any chance make a blunder, to the effect that he has got into the mire. On this account Lukman was surnamed Khattak, and his descendants are known as Khattaks to this day.

April 1901.

The Mahsud blockade, which has been in force now for about three months, is beginning to tell upon the tribesmen, who are now feeling the want of the supplies they usually obtain from British territory. The blockade, which is effected by means of a cordon of fortified posts (connected by patrols) stretching from the Upper Tochi to Wana, effectually prevents any communication between the Mahsuds and their sympathizers in British territory. The Mahsud Wazirs, who in former years came down in large numbers to British territory in the winter, and while there earned sufficient to supply them with salt and grain for the summer, are now almost at the end of their resources, and see that there is nothing for it but to submit and comply with the terms of Government.

They are consequently actively collecting money among themselves to pay the fine of one lakh of rupees which has been imposed upon them, and are paying in to the various officers deputed to collect the fine amounts aggregating about Rs. 2,000 a day.

It is hoped that the whole fine will be paid within three months and the blockade taken off.

The lesson should be a lasting one, not only to the Wazirs, but to all the frontier tribes, who are mainly dependent upon their intercourse with British territory for their means of subsistence.

October 1901.

His home in Paghman was of the usual Afghan pattern, an open and defensible courtyard surrounded by buildings, the Khan's own residence facing the gateway, with open rooms and balconies in front. There were no glass windows, but at night wooden shutters effectually closed up the front of the dwelling rooms, though they left opportunity for biting draughts through the cracks which separated the ill-fitting boards. The furniture consisted of a chair and a bed, but what was lacking in furniture was made up in carpets. The bazaars of Kabul City are full of the carpets of Turkestan, thick felt "numdahs" from Central Asia, embroidered cloths from Bokhara and many varieties of cloths for fighting the bitter cold.

The central reception room was provided with a square recess in the floor, which was the only fireplace of the establishment. Therein a huge wood fire was lighted, the smoke whereof being left to find its way into the outer air. As the fire gradually reduced itself to a condition of red-hot embers, a four-legged contrivance somewhat like a bed was placed over it, and on this a wide felt cloth was spread, which could be conveniently pulled over the knees of anyone sitting on the edge of the recess.

April 1902.

Proceeding through the valley, which now widened and was plentifully garnished with stunted trees, we met two men of the wildest appearance running in great haste, with the matches of their firelocks kindled and without covering to their heads. They said they were in search of their enemies, who had paid them a visit in the night. We passed each other, and soon after beheld a man running after us. He was also armed with a matchlock. We were at first dubious as to his intentions, but on his overtaking us it proved that he had no other motive than to persuade us to look at a sister who was lying sick in the village to which we were now near. As I had some medical skill we agreed to help him, and, leaving the road, crossed a small, but swiftly running, stream with precipitous banks, which took a difficult path through the hills to the north. We reached his village, a small collection of tumble-down huts surrounded by a high wall, at dusk.

October 1902.

It was decided, accordingly, to send an expedition against Lango, to break up this stronghold of rapine and disorder, and to deprive the robber tribesmen of the support they derived from the aid of a body of disciplined fanatics. The operations, which came to an end on August 24, 1901, were completely successful, though owing to a complication of difficulties they lasted for nearly four months. The mutineers fought well; they were armed with weapons of precision, and were found to be unexpectedly well supplied with ammunition for Martini-Henry and Snider rifles, while the Lango tribesmen were formidable on account of their accomplished treachery. The country would have been in any case a difficult one, even if the resistance had been less vigorous, and the difficulty was increased by an unusually heavy rainfall early in the year. The grass grew thick to a height of from six to nine feet, and the swamps were all full. Then there came an outbreak of small-pox, which seriously crippled the expedition. The British officers, however, both military and medical, showed admirable devotion and resource, and the troops, including Sudanese and other natives, behaved steadily and well.

April 1903.

Previous to the British occupation of the Yusafzai plain, men ploughed their fields with a rifle slung over the shoulder or a sword suspended at the waist, and watched the growth of their crops with armed pickets day and night. Similarly, their cattle never went out to graze except they were protected by armed guards. Happily all is now altered, and the change is appreciated by the mass of the people. The cultivator now casts his seed on ground far away from his village. Children now lead out the cattle to graze, and play on the mounds formerly held by the pickets. Men and women follow the tracks across the desert wastes unhindered and undisturbed, and in their visits from village to village daily perform journeys their grandparents never dreamed of. Old men still delight the youth untutored in the use of arms with the stories of the manly deeds of their fathers.

October 1903.

Yar Muhammad Khan placed sentries on all the cisterns that were supplied by springs, and the water that rose in them was dealt out to the people every twenty-four hours. The bazaars, public squares and mosques were crowded with sufferers imploring the pity of the sirdars as they went by, and begging for food; to prove their misery they laid out before them the corpses of their townsmen who had died of hunger, but the chiefs, reduced to extremity themselves, could only encourage them by words and their own stern resignation. To all these horrors was at length superadded the failure of ammunition. Yar Muhammad Khan, it is true, ordered some to be made, but either the materials were bad or the workmen ignorant, for the powder burned in the cannon and left the ball as it was put in.

April 1904.

As we approached Mat through a gorge which leads into the small valley in which it is situated, we saw a gleam of swords from a small look-out tower situated on a rock at the end of the gorge. We sent on those Khetrans who were with us to reassure the garrison of the little tower, who were blowing the fuses of their matchlocks and making ready for an onslaught from a supposed party of Marri raiders. Only three months before the date of our visit to Mat, twelve Khetrans belonging to that village were grazing cattle in a valley behind the village. The Marris surprised and killed the graziers and carried off 180 head of cattle in sight of the village. The villagers were too few in number to venture down from the ridge on which the village stands to the assistance of their sons and brothers, who were butchered before their eyes.

October 1904.

Akhund Darweza relates that the settlements of the Dilazaks were at that time in the plain of Langar Kot, while those of the Yusafzais were in Hashtnagar. Now because the Dilazaks had seized the plain around Langar Kot, when the cattle of the Yusafzais came to the plain to graze, they used to plunder and lift them. If any of the Yusafzais came to the Dilazaks for the purpose of trade, they used to attack them, and the Yusafzais were thus always sufferers at the hands of the Dilazaks. Malik Ahmad therefore gave as his advice that they should have recourse to the Khakkhai.* Although they had several blood-feuds with the Mahmandzais,* still when they went as supplicants to them the Mahmandzais treated them as brethren and allies. The Gagianis,* however, insisted (as the price of their alliance) that the country of Doaba should be theirs, whilst the Mahmandzais demanded Hashtnagar.

The Tarklanrais* alone did not assist them, but the Utman Khel were on their side and opposed the Dilazaks stoutly. They say that the Utman Khel had prepared buffalo hides, which they carried in front of them in battle, so that arrows had no effect on them.

April 1905.

Ayub Khan had with him when he started from Herat on the 15th June an army of 7,500 men and guns, which he calculated, as he moved forward, would be strongly reinforced by tribesmen and Ghazis. The news of his approach spread rapidly and had the most disturbing effect in Kandahar and its neighbourhood. The Governor's authority daily diminished, and many of the inhabitants left the city. On the 4th July a brigade, under the command of Brigadier-General Burrows, started from Kandahar and reached the Helmand on the 11th, encamping on the left bank of the river opposite Girishk. On the right bank Sardar Sher Ali's troops were located, having with them six guns. Two days afterwards these troops deserted in a body to the enemy, but did not succeed in taking their artillery with them, as Burrows, on perceiving their intention, crossed the river and captured the guns.

October 1905.

While the force was encamped on a hill near Kanreguram an informer came and told the Political Officer that the Shabi Khels had all their cattle hidden in a nullah about seven miles away to the north. For this he received a handsome reward. Although it was the middle of the day and

* Names of tribes.

very hot we started at once for the place. On the way we passed some rice fields which were irrigated from a small stream flowing down the hillside. Near these fields was a tower from which a shot was fired at us as we approached. No one was hit and the man who fired the shot fled before we could get up to the tower, and escaped among the hills. We halted there for a short while and knocked the tower down. Then we went on, and about three o'clock reached the place mentioned by the informer. There were fresh traces of cattle on every side, but evidently their owners had taken them away, for we could not find so much as a single sheep. While we were looking about some shots were fired from a neck between two hills, past which we had come, and at the same moment the informer, whom we had brought with us, fled. Many shots were fired after him, but he was soon out of sight. So we started back to camp, and going by a different route reached it just before sunset.

It was said afterwards that the informer was himself a Shabi Khel and that he had taken care to have the cattle removed before the troops started, and that the whole thing was a trap, and that if we had returned by the same route as we went, the tribesmen, who had collected and made an ambush on that road while we were looking for the cattle, would have given us a very bad time.

April 1906.

There is considerable diversity of opinion as to the country from which this tribe came. They themselves can furnish no information of any value, and all that can be elicited from them is a statement that their remote ancestors who first settled in the valley came from somewhere in the north, whence they were driven down by the pressure from above of invading tribes. Settled as they were in the middle of a community entirely different from them in race and language, it is marvellous that they have managed to maintain their ancestral customs in so complete a state. They seldom, if ever, resort to litigation, as all cases between members of the tribe are settled according to tribal custom by a tribunal consisting of the oldest member of each of the eight subsections, sitting as a court of first instance, and the defeated suitor may, if he chooses, exercise the right of appeal to a court of which every householder is a member.

October 1906.

Kotan, who is usually considered the leading Painda Khel in Udistan, came in to see me. He began a long story about the grievous oppression of the Painda Khels by the local officials. He alleged that his people were so harassed that they had sent him to find out whether they might send in a deputation to petition the Government to arrange for the transfer of Udistan, to the British side of the boundary, and that they were even prepared to find the money necessary to buy their country out of Afghanistan.

In further conversation he admitted that the Painda Khels had not much to complain of, except occasional impressment for labour, and that the Governor was treating them in a most conciliatory manner and had practically promised to wipe out all their past offences if they would behave well in the future; that the five regiments reported last week to have reached Margha had not actually arrived but were merely said to be coming; and finally that he himself intended for private reasons to settle again in British territory and hoped to regain the lucrative position which he used to hold here some ten years ago, where he was looked upon as the leading man of all the Painda Khels (which he is not.)

This last fact probably gives a clue to his real object in coming here: he knows that Firoz Khan is sulking with Government over his lost status and is trying to arrange permanent Wazir headquarters in Udistan. If he succeeds, Kotan will be completely overshadowed and will probably have to come here, where it is not likely that he will get much. Kotan probably thinks that if he can spread the rumour that Government is thinking of taking over Udistan, Firoz Khan will hesitate before arranging headquarters in a place which may lose its chief advantage of being beyond Government's reach.

April 1907.

The matter was discussed at a full jirga of all the tribes. It will be remembered that the Mando Khel had purchased and forcibly taken possession of a piece of land over which the Takhto Khel claimed a right of pre-emption. It was decided that the Mando Khel should be offered the opportunity of deciding the dispute according to the principles of Muhammedan Law and that if they refused to do so, the united tribes should raise an army to evict them. The Mando Khel say that if they had known that there would have been all this trouble, they would never have taken the land, but as they have actually taken possession, Pathan honour forbids their withdrawing now. They have accordingly sent in supplication to three other tribes asking for their assistance. Should it be made worth their while, these tribes will certainly join in, as they have finished cutting their crops and have at present no particular business of their own to attend to.

October 1907.

A jirga of all the Chamkanni sections, except the Khani Khels, visited the Political Agent on Friday. They stated that they were unable to enter the Kurram through fear of being arrested in reprisal for claims against the Khani Khels; that they themselves had no power to compel the Khani Khels to make reparation, but that they were willing to furnish substantial security that neither would they themselves commit any offences nor would they allow the Khani Khels to cross their territory to commit any offences: more than that they could not do. There is no doubt that the statement of these tribes is substantially true: they are no more able to control the Khani Khels than the Massuzais, and experience has shown that pressure brought to bear on them in no way reaches to the Khani Khels. The tribes own the territory bordering on the Kurram from above Kirman to near Shakardarra; and the substantial security given by them ought to induce them to adhere to their promises, and should they do so, it is possible that the Khani Khels may weary of their present attitude.

April 1908.

I am glad that I can say that many of you have done a great deal in the direction of suppressing feuds and factions. Many old differences between families and individuals have been composed, and many of you have, also, by personal efforts assisted in the administration. We have had accordingly the satisfactory result of a marked decrease in crime. At the same time, much remains to be done. It would be invidious on my part to mention families or individuals who are not maintaining the relations with each other which conduce to peace, or who foment factional troubles and intrigues. Such cases are not only a disgrace to those concerned but they directly lead to the spread of feuds and crime among the people in the districts and in some cases are apt to reflect across the border. For this reason we cannot permit such cases to pass without notice, and if they continue those concerned have only themselves to thank if they fall into trouble. I have noticed that it is often these very people who talk most of their dignity. You all know that it is my desire to maintain your dignity and self-respect in every way that I can; but unless you maintain it and have proper regard for it yourselves, what are we to do?

I still see that in many murder cases which come before my notice false charges are made against the relations of the murderer or against others who have had nothing whatever to do with the case. If people come forward and give proper assistance in elucidating the facts, we shall hear less of accusations of bribery against the police.

October 1908.

There was a night attack by the Red army at midnight, the only noteworthy fact about which was that the attackers hopelessly lost cohesion, and failed to arrive anywhere. Until daylight rescued them from their dilemma they wandered aimlessly about a country which they are fond of calling their own, and which they should be presumed to know by heart.

I saw the Red infantry firing at about 1,200 yards at the Blue cavalry, but did not trouble to adjust their sights. This detail also escaped the attention of their officers. To-day the Blue cavalry were banging away at the Red infantry with carbines at a distance of fully 4,000 yards.

April 1909.

Some three years ago a dispute regarding the ownership of some landed property arose between various Shaman Khel Mahsuds. Mir Jang, Lalgul and Makarai fancied they had a prior claim to some land occupied by their cousins Panai, Daulat Khan and Pattarai. To avoid legal formalities and delay they determined to have their cousins murdered. The cousins got wind of their intentions and fled to the Garrarai Mahsuds.

Mir Jang and Co. became *de facto* owners of the property in dispute. Last week Panai and Daulat Khan collected a band of some 100 persons to whom they paid Rs. 2,500, and surrounded the house of Mir Jang and set fire to it. Mir Jang, Lalgul, Makarai, Jabbar and three women perished in the flames. One Jahangir broke out but was instantly shot. Only one member of the family escaped, a man named Jami, who, fortunately for himself, was out for the night on a marauding expedition with some friends. Panai, Daulat Khan and Pattarai have thus regained possession of the property on appeal.

October 1909.

On the night of the 13th March a Hathi Khel sepoy named Gul Janan deserted from the Mirzail post while on sentry-go. It appears that he was induced to do this owing to resentment against certain other men of his village, through whose intrigues he believed that two of his uncles had been imprisoned in a murder case. On the night of the 15th March Gul Janan and some of his relations attacked the village of his enemies in the Bannu District, and shot one woman and wounded five others and one man. Since then he has again visited the village, and getting on to the roof of a house shot a Jemadar of the Border Military Police, and again made good his escape over the border. Unless the tribes through whose territory he passed can be induced to deliver him up for trial he will probably become a dangerous outlaw.

April 1910.

(*Petition and Engagement presented by the Shirani Jirga.*)

Owing to the evil deeds of some of the Shirani bad characters who have committed offences in British territory the officers of Government have shut out the tribe from British territory. We therefore now as representatives of all the Shiranis make the following promises in order to have the blockade raised:—

1. Rs. 3,000 are still due by us on account of compensation for offences committed by the tribe. All the stolen property that can be collected will now be handed over. The Chandwan dam and the water-mill which were burnt and destroyed by our tribe we will reconstruct with our own hands. The balance remaining after deducting value of cattle to be returned and the labour we supply in repairing the dam and rebuilding the water-mill will be guaranteed in cash by a trustworthy surety, resident in British territory, who will pay the amount due within the period of two months. The said surety will make up the sum by levying one anna per rupee on our trade, with, if necessary, the assistance of Government. If, however, we wish the blockade to be raised before tender of security we will place twenty hostages in British territory and the cost of their maintenance will be borne by us so long as they remain under detention.

2. As regards future offences we engage to restore the actual stolen property or to point out the offenders or their property when they come down to the plains and make them over to Government within three months from the date of committal of offences. If we fail to do this the whole tribe will be liable to pay compensation. These terms include the Chuhar Khels. In the same manner we shall be responsible for individuals of other tribes who may be in Shirani limits.

3. We engage to expel outlaws, who having committed offences in British territory, seek refuge in our country. We will send down Mir Khan, the murderer, if he agrees to have his case tried by jirga. As regards the murder of Jhangi Ram, charged against us, we know nothing.

October 1910.

The jirga were invited to state their petitions. Their first request, which they pressed with most insistence, was regarding the surrender of runaway women. Its refusal created considerable clamouring among the gathering. The matter requires some explanation. It must not be imagined that the Afridis were asking for the surrender of women who left the country with their paramours. The Afridis have their own methods of dealing with such cases. The real point at issue in this petition was one affecting the available supply of women for the clan.

Every year a number of women, attracted by the prospect of an easier life in Peshawar either run away, or having come with their friends to sell grass and wood, conceal themselves in the city, preferring private service there to the drudgery and squalor of their life in Tirah or Kajurai. In this way, the tribe annually lose some of their not too numerous women, and in addition to the irritation of offended honour, the family loses a chattel which it could dispose of for a consideration, for among Afridis, as among all the lower clases in and around Peshawar, a woman is as much a marketable commodity as is a rifle or a cow. After the proceedings were over and the jirga had been dismissed, the common men of one or two of the clans started a movement in favour of dispersing and leaving Peshawar in token of their dissatisfaction at the rejection of their petition. Fortunately, the wiser counsels of the elders prevailed, and eventually all agreed to accept the situation.

October 1910.

1. The old man, who had only one eye, was telling stories to the boys in the *hujra.* He said :—"Take my advice. When sahibs come to the jhil to shoot, do not listen to their stories of rewards. Keep out of their way. Once I was grazing my cattle near the water-channel of Alam Khan's mill. Alam Khan's ducks were swimming in the water. A Feringhi came up from the other side, and called out to me to throw a clod at the ducks and make them fly. Without thinking, I did as he bade. Now I have only one eye, and a feud with Alam Khan."

2. The trans-borderer said :—"The hospital in Peshawar is good for men, but bad for women. Three years ago the doctor took a bullet out of my knee and saved me from lameness. Our country doctors could not do that. But last year my wife eloped with a Peshawari barber. My threats frightened him, and he turned her out of doors. Just when I thought I could get level with her she took refuge in the hospital, and the doctor still says she is very ill. This is a farce. The Feringhis do not understand women and the customs pertaining to them."

3. The Shinwari elder said :—"I am glad that the British Government has stopped the arms trade in the Persian Gulf. If it had continued, every youngster in the tribe would have purchased a rifle, and how could I keep them all in hand? How could I stop raiding parties from entering British territory?" An Adam Khel, who was present, said :—"What do you care for the British Government? You are a miser and are glad that the six rifles you bought last year for Rs. 300 each are now worth Rs. 500 each."

4. After he had fastened a medal to every man's breast, the General said :—Officers, Native Officers, Non-Commissioned Officers, and Men! I am

indeed pleased to see you again to-day. I have not forgotten the good work you did in the field, and should occasion arise, you may depend upon me to take you with me again on active service. The photograph which has been taken to-day will always remind me of your great services. I have promised to send a copy to the Commander-in-Chief, who takes a great interest in this Corps."

April 1911.

With regard to the caravans from Afghanistan that are said to be on their way to the Mekran coast in connection with gun-running from Muscat, it is probable that several have made Bam a rendezvous and hence the somewhat alarmist reports from Teheran.

There may quite possibly be 600 men in the neighbourhood of Bam, but the statement that "a much larger force is said to be nearer Baluchistan" may be safely regarded as an exaggeration.

The *kafilas* have necessarily to be kept as small as possible, owing to the difficulty of procuring supplies and even water.

Stretches of desert have to be crossed, and large parties of men and camels cannot be kept together. As there is no danger of interference from the Persians or the Baluch tribesmen, a few score of Afghans can march along quite securely.

The majority of these do not trouble to carry firearms, as they equip themselves with rifles and ammunition from such consignments as have been landed from Muscat and sent inland to Baluch chiefs who are interested in the business.

From Bam the route taken by the traders is south-eastwards through Regan to Bampur in Persian Baluchistan. This is another rendezvous, and it is here that news is received as to the success or failure of gun-running in the gulf of Oman.

April 1911.

1. Who are you and what are you doing here? I am a Shinwari of Loargi, and have brought down eight donkey-loads of snow and charcoal for sale in Peshawar. We have had a severe winter this year and our snow pits are full, so we ought to do well this summer. I served formerly in the army, but took my discharge three years ago, as I could not get on with the Subadar of my company. He is a tyrant, and was always bringing false accusations against me.

2. Are you going shooting to-day? There are plenty of duck, teal, geese, and snipe to be found about here. No, I am a bad shot with a shot gun, so it does not give me any pleasure to creep about waist-deep in the muddy water of a rice field. Next spring, however, if I can spare the time, I hope to get some markhor and oorial shooting on the upper slopes of the Safed Koh.

3. Heavy rain has fallen and is still falling in Tirah. We are in great trouble. All our crops are ruined, and many of our cattle drowned; we shall find it very difficult to make both ends meet. Several houses and caves have fallen in. My grandfather's house collapsed yesterday, and the old man's thigh was broken by a falling beam. He has had bad luck, for during the expedition, three years ago, his tower was blown up, and he had only just finished rebuilding it.

4. A raid took place last night at Landai. The gang consisted of trans-border men, with a few outlaws from British territory. An entrance to the village was effected under cover of the darkness. The villagers tried to summon assistance by beating the alarm drum, but, unfortunately, the wind was in the wrong direction. The signal rockets, too, failed to explode, the powder being damp. After a sharp skirmish the raiders retired in a westerly direction. They had, evidently, not escaped without casualties, as blood stains were found for a considerable distance along their line of retreat.